Not My Time

Gary Pacelli

From the Ashes Publishing—Warwick, NY
Hardcover ISBN: 979-8-9878352-7-2
Paperback ISBN: 979-8-9878352-8-9
eBook ISBN: 979-8-9878352-9-6
Library of Congress Control Number: 2023904609
Title: *Not My Time*
Author: Gary Pacelli
Digital distribution ǀ 2023
Paperback ǀ 2023

Dedication

To my wife, Kristin, my soul mate and best friend, I could not have made it without you by my side. Without you, I would not have even tried. I love you always.

—Gary Pacelli

A special thank you to Shauna for being a leader, stepping out on a ledge, and giving me a chance. Without your confidence in me, I would not be back jumping again. To everyone at Skydive Shenandoah for showing me patience and kindness while I regained my confidence and got back in the air.

—Blue Skies

I wrote this book to highlight my three near-death encounters and their consequences. The term "near-death "does not accurately describe the events. I have been so close to dying on three occasions that I could smell Death's cologne. I should not be alive, but it was "Not My Time."

While Skydiving, Wing-suiting to be exact, my parachute opened "hard," breaking my neck and paralyzing me from the neck down. I was conscious and had five minutes to think about my life and face my Death before the inevitable crash landing; this experience has awakened me to the fragility of life and my duties and responsibilities toward others. I bring you along on my journey through times of extreme danger, hardship, and recovery.

This book travels through the complexity of my mind when I was paralyzed and imprisoned inside my own body. I take the reader along on the challenging journey back to everyday life and the sport of Skydiving, relying on the sometimes funny and always entertaining memories of the relationships and friendships I developed as a Law Enforcement officer. NOT MY TIME highlights my passion for Skydiving and the incredible experiences I have encountered, and we have a good laugh during the trip.

This book will help anyone who has given up or is about to quit. Maybe they can find a little spark of hope after reading my story. A little hope goes a long way; People have done great things with just a little hope. Sometimes, a little hope is all you have and all you need.

"A Champion is someone who gets up when they can't." —- Jack Dempsey

My story will put a smile on your face, make you laugh, and want more.

I wrote this book as if I were telling a story, a simple story, to friends sitting around a fire after an incredible day of Skydiving!

I hope you enjoy it.

Blue Skies,
Gary Pacelli

"Life should not be a journey to the grave with the intention of arriving safely in a pretty and well-preserved body, but rather to skid in broadside in a cloud of smoke, thoroughly used up, totally worn out, and loudly proclaiming "Wow! What a Ride!"
— Hunter S. Thompson

"Many people die at twenty-five and aren't buried until they are seventy-five."
— Benjamin Franklin

"First one to die is a Rotten Egg!"
— Dario

Table of Contents

Chapter 1

I was terrified that the squirrels and birds would peck at me, get inside my suit, and eat me alive. The only comfort I had was knowing that at least I wouldn't feel it.

March 9, 2021, was a beautiful, bright sunny morning in Raeford, North Carolina, just as it had been the day before when I arrived at Skydive Paraclete XP. Spring was in the air, and I was excited to jump at a new drop zone. I had been the only "Fun Jumper "there, and it was obvious that I would not be jumping unless other jumpers showed up. This was my first time at Paraclete. I was unsure of my surroundings and their style of doing things; everyone was professional and pleasant, and the drop zone was immaculate; I was impressed.

I earned my skydiving "A" license at the end of the 2019 season. I spent the entire year of 2020 traveling up and down the east coast with my two jump buddies, Sam Kidstar and Big Rich, and Paraclete was my 11th drop zone to visit. I managed to complete three-hundred-thirty-two jumps up to that point safely. Three-hundred-thirty-two is a small number of jumps; with that number, I had acquired enough knowledge and skill to do some damage if I wasn't extra careful, and I wasn't!

I grabbed my gear and entered a hanger that I thought was for fun jumpers; it was for a group of Army guys out of Fort Bragg that had contracted a plane for the day. I am still unsure of what their jobs were in the Army. I assume they were Special Ops because on the side of their rigs were the letters SOC, which stands for Special Operations Command. No matter, after introducing myself and speaking with them for a little while, they invited me to hitch a ride on their plane.

I explained that I had recently finished my ground school and supervised jumps for wing suiting and that I would be practicing my wingsuit pattern upon exiting the plane. They were cool with that and told me to get out last and deploy my canopy a little high to make sure I made it back to the DZ. I did six jumps that day and met some great people, which is precisely why Skydiving is so awesome. The community is so tiny that wherever you go, you usually run into someone you know, or you meet new people and run into them somewhere else. It had been one of the best skydiving days I have ever had; now, let us get back to where this part of my story begins, March 9, 2020.

As I said, the Sun was bright, not a cloud in the sky, and the winds were perfect. Fun Jumpers had shown up; I should explain what a fun jumper is for those that don't know; it's precisely what the name says it is, a skydiver that is not a student, instructor, or military, a skydiver that jumps, for fun.

This day I would be wing suiting; I began to suit up but had this uneasy feeling; the wingsuit was too tight, I felt rushed, and I couldn't pinpoint the source of my anxiety. I couldn't put my finger on the cause, but the feeling kept gnawing at me. I have felt this feeling before, I'm a retired Detective, and I used to call it my Spidey senses. As I continued to suit up, the feeling grew, I considered taking myself off the plane, but my pride and arrogance got the best of me. I had nothing to worry about; I could handle anything. I have a reserve parachute. I'm "Min Diesel." What could go wrong? I'll explain "Min Diesel" later in my story.

I boarded the plane first since I was getting out last and took the 15-minute ride to altitude (around 13,000 ft) with the uneasy feeling growing to the point where I heard in my mind "the voice." The voice we mostly ignore because we write it off as fear; it's not fear. Some say it's your training, and others say it's the Universe or God. Call it what you want; it should not be ignored, and hopefully, by the end of this story, you will know what I believe the "voice" is. The voice in my mind repeatedly told me, "Don't jump; ride the plane down." I ignored it and watched the light by the door turn red; the door opened, the green light went on, and the first jumper checked the spot, set up, and exited.

It's on now, the last chance to ride the plane down. Nope! I get to the door, spot, and exit. Now when you wingsuit, you exit the plane with your arms close to your body; you want to wait a few seconds before you spread your arms and pressurize your suit, so you don't catch the propellor wind and hit the tail of the plane. I exited perfectly when my suit caught air; it made me do a gentle back flip and put me into the perfect body position. It must have looked like I meant to do it if anyone was watching. I followed the pattern I had practiced the day before, and my first unsupervised wingsuit jump was going great.

I have this! This was going awesome. The suit was too short for me and made me fly on an exaggerated head-down angle which meant that I was going super-fast for my 3rd wingsuit jump. "Beep, beep, beep," my helmet altimeter begins to beep at 6,500 ft, time to slow down and deploy my canopy. I reach back, grab my pilot chute, and deploy my main canopy. I immediately realize that I probably should have slowed down a little more, and then "POW," my canopy goes fully open; instantly, it almost sounds like a gun firing, my head snaps back, and I hear this sickening crunch sound and then it feels like someone turned a switch off. I felt this electric charge run from my neck to my toes as my body went limp. The only thing I could move was my head, and I had a little movement in my left hand. I was at around 4,300 ft, totally paralyzed; I could not grab my toggles which meant that I couldn't steer or slow down. My first thought was, "No way, this isn't happening" I gave it a few seconds hoping that the feeling and movement would come back, but it didn't.

I suddenly knew I would die and had the next five and a half minutes to think about it.

Chapter 2

Now, five and a half minutes is both a long time and a flash, it's a long time when you know you're going to die, and you think about how it's going to happen, are you going to get impaled in the trees or drown in a lake, on and on. I died about 1,000 different ways in my mind, but it is a flash when you realize that it is all over in five minutes; after about thirty seconds, you come to terms with it, you give up, accept your fate, and you think about everything you're going to miss and everything that you would do differently. When they say your whole life flashes before your eyes, they aren't kidding. I thought about my wife, Kristin, and my two kids, Chase and Madison, and my two dogs, Gunner and Whiskey, and the best word to describe how I felt was sad, a deep sadness for everything that I would miss and how the world would move on without me.

All this happens fast, then slowly a fire begins to burn inside you, and sadness turns to anger, then anger turns to fury, and I decided that if I were going to die, I would die fighting. I was going to die like a warrior with my sword in my hand. The one thought I couldn't shake looking out into the vast forest around Raeford and thinking that I was going to get hung up in a tree, alive, paralyzed, and no one would be able to find me, and the squirrels and birds would peck at me and get inside my suit, and eat me alive. The only comfort I had was knowing that at least I wouldn't feel it, I guess.

I couldn't shake that thought, but I recently took a canopy course given by a skydiving legend named Kaz Skeekey. She is a badass, she taught me how to steer my canopy using my body weight, so I at least had a tool in my toolbelt, and I was determined to make it back to the drop zone. I began rotating my head and gaining enough momentum to make wide 360-degree turns.

Your mind can be your worst enemy; the thought kept creeping into my head; the other "voice"; it was strong. "Ditch it, ditch it into the trees. Get it over with; even if you survive, you are still paralyzed. That's not living. Your wife and family don't deserve that!" To be honest, it didn't seem like a bad idea at the time. I was in a bad position; if I managed to make it back to the drop zone and survive the inevitable crash landing, I would still have been paralyzed. I probably wouldn't survive the landing, so I didn't have to worry about being paralyzed just yet. During this incident, my GoPro camera was recording video and sound, which is some intense footage.

I kept excellent radio discipline during this accident and did not say a word. My Academy instructors would be proud!

"Death smiles at us all; all we can do is smile back."
— Marcus Aurelius.

So here I am, around 4,000 ft above Raeford, North Carolina, paralyzed from the neck down. I found out later that I had broken my neck, a complete blowout of discs C-5 and C-6. I needed to get as close to the drop zone as possible. All I could do was rotate my head and make wide 360-degree turns, which seemed to be working; I had a few things working in my favor. I had planned my canopy opening in a spot where I knew that if I had a bad main canopy and had to cutaway and go to my reserve, the winds would float my main canopy back to the DZ, and I wouldn't be out a parachute and around $2,500. I was confident that the winds would carry me in the direction of the DZ; I just needed to make my turns so I could burn off altitude and not overshoot the drop zone; if I could stay disciplined, I may pull it off and die close to the drop zone, talk about a rough morning!

I want to clarify; I'm not trying to sound like some tough guy and make you believe that I'm not afraid of death; no one wants to die. I certainly didn't want to, and floating around, unable to move, is terrifying, but this was going to be the second time I was facing my death, so I was no stranger to the Reaper, more on the first close call a little later in the story.

"Don't Fear the Reaper"
—Blue Oyster Cult

The audible altimeter in my helmet beeps at certain altitudes; mine is set for a basic student landing pattern; it beeps once at 1200 ft, twice at 600 ft, and three times at 300 ft.

At this point, you must realize that I was not going for any accuracy landing awards; I was looking to crash and most likely die close to the drop zone so my body could be found; the good thing is that whatever I hit or how hard the impact was, I knew that I had no feeling from the neck down, so it wasn't going to be painful.

"Beep," 1,200 ft; here we go, damn, I'm crossing the runway, I'm going to overshoot the landing zone, and I'm heading for the trees. At least they'll find me. I hope.

"Beep, Beep," 600 ft still heading for the trees, wait, I'm catching a wind, I'm turning!

I have never been very religious; I have always believed in God and tried to do the right thing, and I consider myself a decent human being.

7

"Beep, Beep, Beep," here we go; I'm dead in about 25 seconds; I start to think that many questions I have are about to be answered. I think and say in my mind, "Jesus, please save me." I'm not sure why I thought and said that, but it felt like I needed to, and it was the best decision I ever made.

The wind I caught started to pick up strength, and it was going to put me in someone's backyard directly across the street from the drop zone. That wind put me into a total 180-degree turn, and somehow, I was going to land into the wind, and it might slow me down just enough to survive.

But that's impossible; how does a wind turn you into the wind? You can't have a breeze at your back and one in your face. A tailwind and a headwind? I didn't care. It was working!

"Oh, Shit." I'm not going to clear the chain link fence.

Kaboom, just like the old Batman shows I love watching, I hit the fence just above my knees, it flipped me over, and I hit the ground.

Darkness, silence.

Am I dead?

I feel small.

I try to move, but nothing. I'm alive. I'm paralyzed; I'm screwed.

I didn't know it at the time, but thirty feet to my left was an above-ground pool; had I hit that, I would have drowned. The chain link fence absorbed the impact and saved my life.

Lying there half-faced into the ground with a dark tinted visor, unable to move but alive, I thought I must have broken bones and internal bleeding. I'll take slow, deep breaths until I die; it won't be long now; at least I'm not in pain.

Now on the ground, the military guys noticed that I was flying my canopy very erratically and not where I should have been; they had exited the plane before me and landed quickly, they saw through binoculars that my arms were dangling, and they knew I was in trouble, so they jumped in a truck with a few staff members from Paraclete and followed me till I crash landed, they were there within a minute.

I first saw a tire, then some boots, another tire, and more boots. It was starting to set in, and my worst fear was coming true; I might survive this. I can't live paralyzed; I'm terrified at this point. I feel like I've been imprisoned inside my own body.

I was exceptionally outwardly calm, I knew how much trouble I was in, and my old Marine Corps training kicked in; I "embraced the suck," no point in whining or making a scene. Nothing would change my situation, so I tried to keep my cool and do my best to keep my shit together. I started to freak out a little when they couldn't figure out how to open the visor on my helmet; I asked them to smash it with a rock; I needed air. They figured it out, but I'm a little claustrophobic to this day.

They stabilized me with machine-like precision; they played a significant role in my survival, and I can't thank them enough. Had they not been there, I don't know how things would have turned out. It was another piece of a puzzle that needed to be completed perfectly for me to sit here and write this story.

Now I'm not going to use real names for obvious reasons. The people who showed up saved my life. Paraclete was excellent, and I take full responsibility for my accident; Skydiving is dangerous; it's not golf or bowling; we know the risk; we do it anyway. So, anything I say is not criticism or meant to lessen the fact that I am grateful for everyone that helped me, and at the time, I was either very lucky or very blessed; I didn't know which.

As I said, I was very calm, I had come to realize that I had just had a life-changing event, and I was helpless at that moment to do anything about it. I was also probably in shock.

In Skydiving, you owe Beer whenever you do something for the first time and get caught. The day before, I had mentioned to the drop zone manager that it was the first time I had jumped at Paraclete. Bingo, I owed a case of Beer, and I had it in my truck. It's funny where your mind goes during a traumatic event; they are working on me, saving my life, and I'm worried about paying my Beer fine. That's how your mind tries to protect itself by taking you away from the reality or urgency of your situation.

As they were stabilizing me, they needed to grab my wallet and gather my gear, so I told them to make sure they took the case of Beer out of my truck, so it didn't get wasted. While the paramedics were busy shredding my rig and wingsuit to pieces, one of the staff members from the DZ said to me, "Gary, I've seen this before; football players get it all the time; it's called a stinger, in a day or two you'll get your feeling back." I liked that idea. The other staff member had found my GoPro on the ground, and he had this look on his face like Gollum in the Lord of the Rings when he finally got the ring back. I didn't care, but he mumbled something under his breath as he walked away to play with my GoPro, his" Ring of Power." I'm a huge "Lord of the Rings" fan.

"No, it isn't," he said; he didn't think I could hear him.

I did; boy, did I hear him!

For the next two months, I spent in the Hospital trying to stay positive, I hung on to the "stinger" idea, but I would always hear that voice, "No, it isn't." The idea of it just being a stinger gave me a little hope, and a little hope goes a long way; people have done great things with just a little hope; sometimes, it's all you have and all you need.

At this point, things started to get blurry; I think I started nodding in and out of consciousness; I'm not sure how I got transported across the street to the drop zone where the medevac helicopter landed; these guys were all business. They prepped me and told me that they decided to bypass the trauma hospital in Fayetteville and were taking the twenty-three-minute ride to a hospital in Raleigh, N.C. They explained that this Hospital was better equipped for my injuries. They loaded me into the Helicopter, and now, being unable to move and being placed in it was intense. I had about eight inches of space from my nose to the roof. Honestly, if I hadn't given up all hope of living a normal life, I probably would have been freaked out, but at this point, I didn't care; I considered myself no different than a sack of meat. I even asked the flight paramedic if he could throw me out the door when we got to altitude, "not on my watch!" he replied. He didn't see the humor in my request!

Note: If you are ever unlucky enough to be loaded onto a medevac chopper, CLOSE YOUR EYES! I'm still pulling dirt out of my eye sockets.

I didn't realize it at the time, but so many amazing things that were all pieces to a puzzle that had to be completed for me to survive, recover, and thrive had occurred; I will go into detail later in the story. If even one of these events/pieces did not happen, I would have either been dead or permanently paralyzed from the neck down.

I landed at the Hospital exactly twenty-three minutes later; as I said, this medevac crew was no joke, great job. Next thing I know, I'm getting rolled out and into the Hospital, but I swear there must have been at least twenty doctors, nurses, and technicians working on me and probably another ten standing by. I thought, man, something terrible must have happened; I wonder what they are waiting for to come in. I asked the nurse doing my intake as others were putting IVs in me; they were even X-raying me as we were running down the hallway; actually, they were running down the hallway; I wasn't running anywhere, ever again, I thought. I asked the intake nurse, "what's going on? Did something happen?" she smiled at me and said, "you, you happened!" I realized at that moment that I was in good hands; these people gave a shit; I couldn't figure out why? I was finished; what was the point? Just throw me in the corner and leave me be. I was hideous.

They must have scanned me with the portable X-ray machine about four times. They checked every inch of my body and could not understand how I didn't have any broken bones or even a scratch on me. I thought I had to be all busted up inside, but nothing.

Chapter 3

And that is all she wrote: bye-bye, off to wonderland! And none too soon.

I don't know what they hit me with, but the next ten days are all compressed and jumbled up; I will do my best to describe the significant events as I remember them happening, but as I said, everything is a little hazy.

Before this, I had at least eleven surgeries from a previous incident where some shitbag tried to murder me on a highway, but I will get into that later. However, I do not believe that when someone gets operated on that, they should spend their time in the Hospital in extreme pain. And honestly, they knew what they were doing; I had managed to keep it together until this point, but I think that was because my brain was occupied, and I didn't have time to think about my situation. I can say without a doubt that I would not have been able to hold it together without being heavily medicated. Even the best hospitals can be terrifying, especially at night, and especially if you can only feel or move your head. Also, I was in North Carolina and lived in Upstate New York.

This road I was going down, I would have to go down alone but hey, as one person told me

"What were you thinking? You got what you deserved," and I didn't want anyone to see me anyway.

I was alone; wait, stop.

Yes, I was alone in the Hospital, but I wasn't alone.

My wife, Kristin, is the nicest person I have ever met. We met when we were teenagers and up to that point were together for thirty-three years. Kristin is a 3rd-grade schoolteacher and has always supported me and my insanity. We are opposites, and where I can be intense and relentless at times, Kristin is calm and soothing; the combination has worked well for us, and I'm learning to be in the moment and just "let it be."

Kristin was at work when she got "the call," She had just dismissed her class for lunch when her phone began to vibrate. Oh, it must be Gary, she thought. We spoke every day when she had lunch; Kristin looked down to see the phone number, Paraclete, N.C. that is weird, she thought, Gary's phone must be dead, or something terrible happened. Stop. Gary's fine.

Kristin: Hello

Caller: Hi, is this Kristin Pacelli?

Kristin: Is he dead?

Caller: No, he is not

Kristin: Oh my God, what the fuck happened?

Kristin walks across the hall where her three teacher friends are waiting for her to have lunch. She is looking for a pen to start writing notes down.

Caller: He was wing suiting and had a hard opening; he is being flown out on a medevac helicopter. We think he snapped his neck, we got to him fast, and we noticed that his arms were dangling; he might have been unconscious, but we are not sure. We followed him until he landed, and the Army Medic stabilized him immediately.

Kristin drops to her knees, overwhelmed, head spinning; what do I do now? Where do I start? The caller is one of the top staff members at Paraclete; we will call him Kevin (not his real name).

Kevin gave Kristin his cell phone number and explained that he had gathered all my gear and sent my wallet and shoes along with me to the Hospital. Kevin said that he would update Kristin as he got more information and not to worry about my truck and gear, he would secure everything, and Kristin could keep the truck there as long as needed. Kristin hung up, walked into an empty, dark classroom, sat on the floor, and began crying. Word spread throughout the school like wildfire; her principal entered the room, sat down, and began to cry with her. she then sent her home; Kristin needed to pick the kids up and let them know I had been in an accident. Now that I think about it, I had it easier.

Kevin was very professional, a man of his word, and he kept in touch. He was a tremendous help, and I say, Thank you.

Kristin's worst nightmare had come true; where did she even begin? She couldn't jump on a plane to North Carolina; we had two kids in school. This happened during Covid; none of the drop zones allowed spectators, so Kristin had never been to a drop zone; she didn't know the people or even the language we use. Kristin immediately called the Hospital in Chappel Hill, N.C., that she was told I was going to. And they didn't have any info on me yet; Kevin had no idea that the Medevac diverted and took the long ride to the Hospital in Raleigh. She couldn't speak to me and didn't know I wasn't there. Suddenly Kristin remembered that my partner when I was assigned to narcotics, Big Lenny (real name), had recently moved to South Carolina. She immediately called him, and he set out to find me.

Big Lenny was driving with his wife Lisa when he saw Kristin Pacelli's phone info come across the info screen on his vehicle; he looked over to Lisa and said, this can't be good. He thought, why would Kristin be calling him? Why would Kristin be calling him at 1:00 in the afternoon? He knew she should be working. He answered the phone, and he was right; it wasn't good; Kristin was crying. A lot, and he could barely understand what she was saying. Kristin finally calmed down enough to give the information as she understood it. He immediately dropped Lisa off at home and began the four-hour ride to the Hospital in Chappel Hill, North Carolina.

So, Here I am, in the trauma ICU, scared, hopeless, high as a kite, waiting for the neurosurgeon. I turn my head to the left and back to the front, and I think, I'm whacked out of my mind; I just saw Big Lenny standing there. I look again, and he is still there; I laugh a little. I look again, and Lenny's still there; I'm not hallucinating! Damn, it was good to see him, he told me about his adventure of being sent to the wrong Hospital and trying to find me, and I got to speak to Kristin. I lied; I told her I was OK and not to worry, I was going to be OK, "it was just a Stinger," "no, it isn't!" I hear him say that every time!

Every time I think, or hope, that it's going to get better miraculously, I hear his voice: "No, it isn't, that prick. Sorry, he was a good guy, but at the time, well, you can imagine.

I apologized to Kristin; I felt like such a loser. I have never felt so ashamed. I promised her that I was going to walk out of that Hospital; somehow, someway, I was going to make it happen.

It was good to see Big Lenny, but I could see the look on his face; I was in serious trouble, and it was sinking in. Lenny left and went and cleaned out my hotel room in Fayetteville; it was in a rough part of town. When I traveled for Skydiving, I always tried to get the cheapest hotel room because all I do is sleep and shower there. I had no idea it was that bad until the nurse told me they called it Fayetnam!

The nurse began prepping me for an MRI and getting me ready for my surgery; at the time, I didn't know how important it was to get into surgery as quickly as possible.

I began to think about what life would be like being a quadriplegic,

Quadriplegic: A person affected by paralysis of all four limbs.

The thought was maddening; I knew I couldn't do it. I couldn't bear to think about putting Kristin and the kids through having to take care of every need I would have, feeding me, bathing me, dressing me, everything.

I thought about how I would end it. My current situation meant I had few options; I remembered the movie Silence of the Lambs when Hannibal Lecter convinced the lunatic in the next cell to swallow his tongue and kill himself.

That's the answer; I will swallow my tongue,

Oh, the magic of Hollywood; after trying to swallow my tongue for about thirty minutes, I only got the one thing on my body I could feel, my tongue to hurt.

I would have to wait until I got released, and I would get a motorized wheelchair and drive it in front of a bus or a train, how about a fuckin missile!

This is the stupid stuff you think about when you lose hope, and your mind becomes your enemy.

The thought of being a quadriplegic was terrifying; it felt like being imprisoned in your body, like your body was a coffin. I felt tiny inside my own body.

The Doctor showed up and introduced himself; I will call him Dr. Bagin. Dr. Bagin was excellent, he looked to be in his mid-forties, healthy, and confident, and I got a perfect vibe from him. I found out later that he was probably one of the best neurosurgeons on the east coast and just happened to be in the Hospital that day, more puzzle pieces. He explained that from the X-ray, he could see that discs C5 and C6 had completely blown out, and with some luck, since they crumbled, they probably didn't sever my spinal cord, but he needed an MRI to be sure.

He was sending me for an MRI, then right into the operating room. The only problem with that plan was that there was no way I was getting in that MRI tube. They would have to put my head in some wooden contraption to keep it from moving. I already felt like I was inside a coffin in my own body; there was no way I could handle getting in that tube, not after what I had just gone through.

Here we go, more drugs! Hurray! I think it was valium, a lot of it; I was in and out of consciousness, like watching pictures flash on a screen. Whatever it took, give me everything you have; I was no longer trying to be a hero this day.

That is how it went; Dr. Bagin replaced two discs in my neck with titanium cages and a plate and cleaned out the wreckage from my old discs. I woke up back in the trauma ICU, and It seemed like days before I saw him again and got the results of the MRI and surgery. As I said, I was on some serious drugs. I know now that Dr. Bagin had contacted Kristin immediately after surgery, but I had no way of speaking to her yet; even if I knew where my phone was, I couldn't hold it or dial it.

It seemed like days, and it might have been before I saw Dr. Bagin; let me rephrase that. I'm sure I saw him at least the next day, but I don't remember it. The important thing is that my spinal cord did not snap; it was severely bruised and swollen. Dr. Bagin explained how lucky I was; he said two more hours and I would have been paralyzed from the neck down for the rest of my life. He said that they were going to keep me in the trauma ICU for a little while so they could monitor me. Good news, but it's hard to see the good when you cannot move, so back in my head I went; I sat there for a long time, thinking all the "what if's," driving myself crazy with doubt and negativity.

How did I get here?

Did I get what I deserved?

Why did I even start skydiving?

I was starting to understand what the popular Skydive saying, "Blue Skies, Black Death," meant. It's hard to imagine how an activity that brings so many people such peace, tranquility, and spiritual experiences can cause so much pain and destruction.

Chapter 4

On July 18, 2003, my group and I were following a person suspected of being in New Jersey from Virginia to pick up a load of cocaine; this was day two of our surveillance. At this time, I was assigned to the Drug Enforcement Administration as a Task Force Officer (TFO) to Group 9, Paterson Post of Duty (POD). This day was a beautiful summer day; it started out uneventful. We surveilled the target from Fort Lee, NJ., over the George Washington Bridge into Washington Heights in New York City.

We followed him as he drove from Bodega to Bodega, doing nothing exciting except driving, parking, and talking on his cell phone. It was Friday; Fridays in the summer were federal holidays, Federal Fridays, and it was tradition to wrap up whatever you were working on by noon and head to the Bar by 2:00. Well, it wasn't a federal holiday. Still, to our group, it certainly was treated as one.

We would never wrap up an active job to go hang out in a bar, but we knew the target had paid with cash for his hotel room till Monday. "Through our experience and training," we also knew that there was no way this person would pick up a load of coke on a Friday and then go sightseeing in New York City all weekend with his girlfriend.

"Through our experience and training," Ha! That is the most overused sentence used in Law Enforcement; I had to throw it in there!

20

No way, no how. The target would be too worried about getting robbed; he would pick up that load and head straight down the Turnpike, affectionately known as the Black Dragon by the New Jersey State Police. Furthermore, we knew he had the hotel room till Monday checkout, and us following him around with ten undercover vehicles was starting to look like a parade or a funeral procession. It doesn't take a counter-surveillance expert to realize you are being followed, and we ran the risk of blowing the whole job. I called my supervisor and friend, Joe (not his real name), and gently reminded him of the holiday and suggested that he pull the units off and leave a skeleton crew to follow this guy around lightly, and we could break off. Sgt. Joe declined my suggestion and gave it the predictable, let's give it one more hour routine.

Here is a little more background on my Law Enforcement experience up to this point. I had been very fortunate. I had some significant assignments; I started as a corrections officer for the Passaic County Sheriff's Department. After graduating from the corrections academy, I returned to the police academy. After graduation, I was placed on County Patrol and then transferred to the motorcycle squad. I was on the Motorcycle squad for around ten years and worked my way up to Corporal and was second in command of the unit; after that, I went to work as a Detective for a small municipal town, the town that I grew up in. I worked there for around three years until I returned to the Sheriff's Department as Detective first grade assigned to the DEA as a Task Force Officer (TFO). I was also assigned to the Passaic County Prosecutors Office Narcotics/Gang Task Force. I was on the Sheriff's Emergency Response Team (SERT), an Underwater Search and Rescue Diver, and a Police Academy Drill Instructor. I was a busy guy, but we also liked to have a good time and break each other's chops.

Everyone I worked with was usually huge, over 6 feet tall, and built like a tank. I'm smaller, so I had to have some thick skin. For example, the first day I reported for duty at the motorcycle garage, they posted a sign on the column next to my bike that read, "You must be this tall to ride this ride." Of course, the line was about two inches higher than the top of my head. Just like at an amusement park, fantastic, that was pretty creative. Now, I could give it as well as I could take it. When I got to narcotics, as I said, everyone was a giant, some real freaks of nature, and every time we went out on a job and had to get physical, I'll give you one guess who the bad guys always wanted to fight, me! And I would always give them what they wanted. A prosecutor's office lieutenant nicknamed me "Min Diesel," he said that I looked like Vin Diesel, so he called me Min Diesel, the Short and Furious, instead of Fast and Furious. All said and done, I worked with some great guys, and I really miss it.

Back to July 18, 2003, during the next hour, the whole mood of the job changed. I was parked on a side street in Washington Heights and stuck out like a sore thumb; I knew things had changed. I started to get that uneasy feeling. My Spidey senses were screaming. The target began to move; he started heading back to Jersey. My Sgt. got on the radio and ordered whoever was behind the target vehicle to pull him over and identify him after he made a U-turn heading toward his hotel.

That was a bad move. We were technically "undercover"; we were not dressed for a motor vehicle stop, and we would have to devise a believable reason for pulling the suspect vehicle over. We always ran the risk of spooking the target and blowing the entire job. I called the sergeant to find out why we were doing this, and he explained that the Group Supervisor wanted an identification on the target and that the Fort Lee Police Department didn't have a marked unit available to make the stop and identify the suspect, so we must do it ourselves.

It figures some desk jockey sitting in his office in Newark wanted to be relevant, so he gives an order that goes against all our training and common sense.

But none of us were surprised!

Remember that we are in shorts and t-shirts in undercover vehicles; it's just not a good idea. As luck would have it, we hit construction coming back over the bridge, and all the units except for me got held back, or they just lost us. As we made the U-turn and got back on Route 4 heading towards the hotel, I activated my hidden emergency lights and gave a quick chirp of my siren, and the suspects, gold-colored Cadillac, pulled over to the shoulder.

I took my badge, hanging on a chain around my neck, out from under my shirt, and I walked up to the driver's side window; I was wearing shorts and a sleeveless T-shirt. I identified myself to the driver and asked for his driver's license, he held it close to his chest, and as I went to grab it, I made a rookie mistake; as I went to grab the license, he pulled it in, and I reached into the car to grab it. As I reached in, I instantly noticed that the vehicle was in drive and the driver had his foot on the brake, our eyes met, and he hooked my arm under his arm and slammed down on the gas. Off we went; I was running to try and keep up with the car, but he was accelerating. If I fell, I would get run over by his back tires, so I dove into the vehicle; I was in the car a little more than waist deep, and my legs were dangling out the driver's side door. I looked over my shoulder and saw that we had just crossed into the middle lane, and he was heading towards the concrete divider; he was going to squash me like a bug. I hear this voice, like a roar inside my head, "shoot him, Shoot him Now!"

Bang!

Next thing I know, I'm violently tumbling down the fast lane of Route 4 in Fort Lee on a beautiful summer day. Time slows down during stuff like this, and I remember thinking, will I ever stop?

When I finally came to a stop, I was on my knees in the fast lane facing oncoming traffic, looking down with my weapon still in my hand; I looked up to see a tractor-trailer heading right for me. As I said, everything is in slow motion, and I think, what's next? Will a piano fall out of the sky and land on my head?

Right before impact, I get yanked out of the way of the truck. My partner Big Lenny had shown up just as the suspect took me for the ride. Big Lenny had no idea what exactly happened; he heard the shot but didn't know if I got shot or if I shot the driver. He asked if I was OK. My response was I'm OK; get that motherfucker! He jumped in his SUV and began to chase him.

I was so embarrassed and pissed. I don't remember pulling my weapon, but it was right there in my hand, I heard the shot, but the driver kept going; no way that I could have missed him. All these thoughts were going through my head as I walked up the shoulder of the highway; I was talking to myself, I was pissed, and I was all messed up with a concussion. Traffic was at a dead stop at this point. As I walked to my vehicle, bleeding from road rash, scraped up, banged up, and talking to myself with my weapon out, I remember saying, "I'm gonna kill that motherfucker!"

At that moment, I noticed the vehicle right next to me; windows rolled down. I saw a typical family, a father driving, two kids in the back seat, and the mother in the front passenger seat, our eyes locked on one another. I saw this absolute look of horror in her eyes, and then it hit me. Holy shit, she's terrified; she's terrified of me!

I'm talking to myself, bleeding with my weapon in my hand. I quickly holstered my weapon, made my way to my vehicle, got in, started laughing, and then drove down the shoulder and tried to get on the pursuit.

When I fired my weapon, I struck the driver in the chest on an angle, and the bullet went through his chest and lodged in his right elbow. He turned the steering wheel sharply to the right, which tossed me out. Big Lenny chased him to the George Washington bridge's lower level, where he rammed the vehicle. Another group member showed up, and they began ordering the driver out of the car. They couldn't see inside the vehicle because the windows were covered with blood. Like in the movie, "Pulp Fiction," the driver's door opens, then closes a few times, and they are about to light the car up. Finally, the door opened, and the driver slumped out; he had lost so much blood that he couldn't undo his seatbelt. They did what they had to, stopped the bleeding, and saved his life. I went to the bridge's upper level and never caught up with them. Which was probably a good thing for both of us. When I returned to the original scene of the shooting, I surrendered my weapon to my Chief, and Lenny and I were immediately taken to the Hospital by my Sergeant. That's where I met the man in the nice suit.

We got out of the car and walked to the entrance to the Hospital. The man in the suit says to me, are you Gary Pacelli?
Me: who are you?
Suit: I'm your lawyer; give me your phone. You speak to no one; all your calls go through me. You don't even talk to your doctors. Understand?
Me: yes.
Suit: where is your wife?

Me: Home, pregnant, on bed rest.

Suit: She doesn't watch TV, answer the phone, or answer the door. Since she is on bed rest, we can't put her in a helicopter and bring her here, so who can we send there to stay with her?

Me: Jose's wife, Jose is in Miami on a job, but he lives close to me, and Daisy should be home.

OK, so you get the idea of how this is turning out; my Union Delegate had hired the attorney as soon as it went over the radio, Big Lenny called a 10:13 Officer-involved shooting with an Officer down.

When a 10:13 is called, it is a big deal; radio traffic stops, except for essential personnel with relevant information. All available units converge on the scene from all surrounding Departments. This was going to be a complicated scene involving multiple jurisdictions, Municipal agencies, three county Agencies, State Police, and the Drug Enforcement Administration were all involved. And the shooting was all over the news already; Route 4 ended up being shut down for six hours in both directions, it was about to get worse, and we all knew it.

Back home, my wife, Kristin, answered the phone and watched TV; who wouldn't? My son was about to be born any day, and she was on bed rest; this was the last thing she needed going on.

I remember being in the Hospital with Lenny, my Lawyer, the Sheriff, the Chief, the Sergeant, Internal Affairs, and my PBA Reps; they were in a heated argument with Bergen County homicide; Bergen County Homicide demanded that I give a statement. No way was that going to happen. We were told Sharpton was on the way. A member of the DEA Shooting Team from Washington, DC., was already there. The news kept reporting on the shooting nonstop. I looked over to Lenny and said, "man, we're screwed" Lenny Looked at me and said," No,

26

Bud, you're screwed." Kristin didn't believe I was OK, considering the situation. All this was happening at once, and the stress level was off the charts when they suddenly interrupted right in the middle of the news reporting on the shooting.

Breaking News!

Koby Bryant has just been charged with Rape.

Sorry Kobe, better you than me. There was a loud cheer, and we were all clapping and high-fiving. The news dropped the story and never reported on it again. My uncle worked for NBC, and he got me the tape of the final newscast. I used to have a picture of Koby Bryant hanging in my basement.

I got released from the Hospital. I was OK until the adrenaline wore off about a week later, and I couldn't even get out of bed. My son was born, and we named him Chase; like a police chase, it seemed appropriate.

The suspect admitted trying to crush me against the divider and was charged with attempted murder of a police officer and held on a 2-million-dollar bail. He sued everyone; He sued me for twenty-five million. The suspect claimed that he didn't know I was a Cop and thought that I was carjacking him, even though they found his driver's license on the road. He then changed his story. He said that I walked up to the car and shot him, they cut him a deal, he dropped all the lawsuits, and they gave him lifetime probation. What a joke. It wasn't personal, though.

I was forced to retire and had eleven surgeries and countless procedures over the next five years; I had six rotator cuff surgeries on my left shoulder before they replaced it with titanium on the seventh operation, then my deltoid muscle snapped and had to be reconstructed. The doctor went back in one more time when he thought the shoulder replacement was infected. I also had two lower spine surgeries; they replaced two discs with titanium cages and finished me off with a left wrist surgery. Eleven surgeries and the doctor doesn't even send me a Christmas card; that's not true; my shoulder surgeon is a good friend. His wife was Kristin's college roommate.

I was awarded a Meritorious Service Award and two of the highest medals in Law Enforcement, The Legion of Honor and The Combat Cross. I was pretty messed up for a long time, but I always wondered about "the voice" that saved my life that day, was it my training? Was it God? At the time, I wasn't sure.

I put on around 75 lbs. during the five years I was operated on. I went back to work a few times, instructing at the academy and doing surveillance for private investigators. I even got hired by the FBI as an Investigative Specialist to do surveillance full-time, I worked out of Federal Plaza in New York for about a year, but it was different. I always told myself that I would skydive if I got back in shape. I had done a static line jump out of a Cessna in 1987, and it was a great goal to motivate me.

It took me almost five years, but I got down to 175 lbs. from 260 lbs. I went and got my Skydiving license. Skydiving had everything I was looking for, the comradery, the equipment, the training, and the adrenaline.

Chapter 5

I opened my eyes; oh damn, I'm still here. I must have dozed off; I was dreaming and forgot where I was. I was in the Hospital, paralyzed. What the hell was I going to do?

I have to try and move; I had to move. I concentrated on every muscle in my body.

Could it be?

I thought that I was moving my right big toe. I yelled for the nurse; she opened the curtain. I told her that I felt I was moving my right big toe, she didn't see it, but she ripped off my sock and grabbed my toe; I was trying so damn hard. "I feel it," she yells. She leaves to get the Doctor.

Dr. Bagin came, felt the slight movement in my toe, and looked genuinely happy. This was huge, and this scene played out three more times over the next four days. My left big toe, right index finger, and left index finger. All these movements had to be felt; they could not be seen. Dr. Bagin then told me, "I have done everything that I could do; the rest is up to you; there is no reason why you can't recover if you put the work in. If you put the work in, there is no reason why you can't skydive again." He then told me how lucky I was that my discs crumbled under the impact, and had they stayed intact, they would have snapped my spinal cord; he called my injury an incomplete spinal cord injury.

Wow, talk about an overdose of hope; I could move the four furthest points on my body very slightly. I was off to the races, and from that moment on, everything changed. I started to reflect on all the things that had gone right and not get stuck on all the things that had gone wrong. I graduated, I could now go to a room outside of the ICU, then after that, I could start physical therapy, but that was still a long way off, and I had to decide whether I would stay in North Carolina or go home to New York for treatment. The hospital I was in is well known throughout the country for its physical therapy wing, but New York was my home; I could be close to my family.

I got transferred to a regular floor in the Hospital; it was a little scary, I'm not going to lie. I had just gotten comfortable in my little corner of the ICU; the nurse's station was ten feet away and was busy, noisy, and crowded. There was a lot for my mind to focus on when I wasn't nodded out in my drug-induced hallucination/dream state; I saw no reason to leave.

Couldn't I live in this little corner of the ICU while the world forgot about me, and I wouldn't have had to face the enormity of the task at hand? Like the Doctor said, it was up to me; at this point, I wasn't sure if I had it in me.

There was no backup available.

Help was not coming.

Holding the line was not good enough; I had to advance. The odds were against me, I was at rock bottom with nothing to lose, and I only had one shot at the title; this one was for all the marbles.

"A Champion is someone who gets up when they can't."
—Jack Dempsey.

I was about to see what I was made of; I had a good idea, having been through Marine Corps boot camp at Parris Island S.C., the Corrections Officer Academy, and a Police Officer Academy. I spent years screaming at people as a Police Academy Drill Instructor, teaching recruits never to give in and to fight till the lights went out, teaching them to reach inside and light the fire of their soul when they thought they could not take it anymore.

It was my turn now,

Again!

I needed to remember who I was and whom I was fighting for; I also had to accept and believe that if God went through all the trouble to save my stupid ass, he wouldn't just leave me hanging now when things would be at their most challenging. I mentioned that I wasn't a religious person; I had read the Bible; I can't say that I understood most of it, and I can't quote you any verses, but I think that I retained what I needed to up to this point in my life and the one verse that kept me motivated and in the fight was:

"If God is for us, who can be against us?"

The hardest part for me wasn't believing that I had asked to be saved and was saved.

Or that way, too many things had to happen for me to be alive, and God had intervened.

No, I was OK with accepting that.

I had a hard time believing that I deserved or was worthy of being saved.

I didn't go to church; I wasn't volunteering at food banks or hospitals.

I was a Cop for many years and worked in narcotics; narcotics is probably the roughest, dirtiest division in law enforcement. We never broke the law, but we certainly weren't saints.

We were fair.

I struggled and still struggle with the why? Why me? Was there something that I was supposed to do? Save a cat out of a tree? Turn the corner, see a building on fire and run in and save a family? Or say a kind word to a stranger on the street at their wit's end and about to give up? I will never know, and I've learned to accept what is and be thankful for it. I try to live my life in a way worthy of being saved and for what has been done for me.

Lenny was the most competent Detective I had ever worked with; he was street smart and book smart; if you were working with him, he expected competence, and there were no cutting corners. This was great for me. When I began working with the narcotics unit, I was way out of my league; I was an excellent Detective, but I had never worked at this level, and we were doing some big jobs.

The Passaic County Sheriff's Department, under the newly elected Sheriff. Sheriff Jerry Speziale teamed up with the Passaic County Prosecutor's Office under Prosecutor Avigliano; they put together the Passaic County Narcotics and Gang Task Force. All sixteen towns from Passaic County were asked to assign personnel to the Task Force. The task force was set up with different levels of squads or groups, starting with street-level narcotics sales, then mid-level and high-level. I had just done an inter-governmental transfer from the Wanaque Police Department back to the Passaic County Sheriff's Department and was assigned to the high-level narcotics unit. The members of this group were also farmed out and on loan to the Drug Enforcement Administration. We handled Cartel level narcotics activity and money laundering. I was extremely fortunate to be partnered up with Big Lenny and his primary partner, my friend Jose; I learned so much, fast; the jobs we were doing were high-speed and extremely dangerous, and there was no room for error. I was picked explicitly for that unit because when I resigned from the Sheriff's Department three years earlier, the new Sheriff was my old partner Jose's narcotics partner, and he loved how I left and "stuck it to the man," and Jose also requested me.

I remember when I had just started working with Lenny, we rolled up on someone that we knew had an outstanding court warrant for his arrest, he saw us as we rolled up, and he started running. I went to jump out of the car to chase him when Lenny stuck his arm out and stopped me. Lenny says we only run when we have to, watch and learn! The dude is running down the street, right down the middle of the road. Lenny calmly but deliberately follows him with the SUV we were in, gets right up next to him, swings the driver's side door open, and hits him with it, not hard, but hard enough. The guy goes down and tumbles a few times, and Lenny calmly cuffs him and puts him in the back seat. He looks at me, smiles, and doesn't say a word. That's experience.

When I initially resigned from the Sheriff's Department and went to work with JP for Wanaque, I told no one. I couldn't; if the administration at the PCSD thought that anyone of my friends knew that I was resigning and didn't rat me out and tell the Sheriff, they would be destroyed.

Jose was mad at me initially for not telling him, but once they started interrogating him, he understood and thanked me.

I worked Patrol in Wanaque for around eight months when a spot in the Detective bureau opened; no one put in their resume for it; they didn't want it, and that should have been a red flag for me. The Chief called me in and told me to put my resume in, so I did. Once I put my resume in, other people wanted it, of course. The Chief stood his ground and gave the spot to me. A promotion like that is a big deal in a small town, and it had to be voted on by the town council. I was approved and reported to the Bureau.

I grew up in this town, lived there, and went to high school with most of the people who worked for the Department. I was about to understand why no one wanted the slot in the detective bureau.

I reported for my first day of work, I already had eleven years of experience, and I met my new Sergeant, Let's call him Sgt. Smith (Not his real name). Smith showed me my desk and began reading me the riot act. He explained that he didn't like the Passaic County Sheriff's Department and was against "Jack," Chief Reno hiring me. Smith explained that "He" was the Sgt. and that I worked for him, not with him. He then told me that his wife was a teacher like mine and that it was all about him," I would never get a day off when school was out, and my wife was off work, so don't ask. There were only two of us, him and I, that was it.

Smith told me that he understood I had eleven years of experience, but he didn't care. "I don't care what you did in Paterson or Passaic; that doesn't matter; this is Wanaque!" I had enough at this point and said, "I get it; these are the mean streets of Wanaque," I grabbed my radio and walked out.

Why me? Why do I always have to work for lunatics? That is how it went. I was aggressive and did my job exactly the way the Chief wanted me to. Sgt. Smith could have sat back; I made him look good, but he was too insecure and couldn't do it. Smith spent the next three years driving himself crazy, trying to get me in trouble; he couldn't touch me. I just did almost ten years under a tyrant at my old department.

We used to participate in the Polar Plunge to raise money for the Special Olympics. Most of the Department would head down to Point Pleasant, NJ, at the end of February; we would all get hotel rooms and usually start drinking around 7 am so we could jump in the Ocean at around 9 am. In February, the Ocean in New Jersey is cold! We would do the plunge and have a massive party in the bar, Jenkins. Cops from all over the state were there. It was really fun. We were usually passed out in bed by 7 pm. I got a call this particular day from my favorite Sgt. Sgt. Smith. He said that he had just got some information that a local heroin dealer whom I had arrested a few times was telling everyone that he knew where my wife and I lived and that he would kill me.

I knew Smith's game by now. He probably had that info for days but just wanted to fire me up when I was having fun. I told him not to bother me with his nonsense and hung up the phone. I went back to sleep, absolutely not worried; I would take care of this when I got home.

I got home and went to work Monday, I sent my informants in and bought heroin from my target, Mr. Kurst, Brad Kurst, and he was the worst. Brad was a small hand-to-hand street dealer from the city of Paterson. Paterson was a city in Passaic County. It was the third largest city in New Jersey; he thought he'd move to Wanaque and openly sell heroin and run the town. That was not going to happen; I had arrested him three previous times already.

I put the work in, did my drug buys, typed up my affidavit for a search warrant, had it reviewed and signed by a judge, and I was ready to go; I just needed one more thing. I had to ditch Sgt. Smith!

I asked the Chief if he could order Sgt. Smith not to participate in the execution of the warrant, The Chief wouldn't do it, but he would give me five minutes, five minutes from the time we breached, to discuss things with Mr. Kurst; ok, I'll take what I can get.

I had mentioned that I went to High School with most of the guys in the Department, so I assembled my team. Me, JP, Sgt. Cavallaro, Sgt, Fackina, and Sgt. Huber; all solid guys. I did the Ops plan, and we decided that since the house was back in the woods with a long driveway, we couldn't come from the front; they would see us coming and quickly dispose of the evidence. This is a small town, so we're not talking about the mother lode. We decided to take the half-mile walk to the back of the house

35

through the woods; they would never expect us from that direction.

We began our trek through the woods as soon as it got dark, and by the time we got near the house, the temperature had dropped significantly, and the snow on the ground had frozen solid. Every step we took sounded like we were walking on Captain Crunch cereal. Finally, we were close enough, and I gave the order to hit the house, Sgt. Cavallaro went in first, and I was behind him. When Sgt. Cavallaro hit the door, he went right through it instead of opening it. Like a "Kool-Aid" commercial. I was right behind him, and as I entered the house, I looked to my left, and there was Mr. Kurst, sitting there on a couch with a deck of heroin in his hand.

Now the Chief was true to his word, he held Smith back for five minutes, and by the time he arrived, we were categorizing evidence and finishing up. Smith was visibly pissed. Mr. Kurst must have slipped when we arrived and was slightly banged up. We finished up and brought our suspects and evidence back to headquarters. Smith wouldn't stop. He kept asking me," Hey Gar, what happened to Brad? You can tell me he deserved it."

I replied, "I don't know, I didn't see it. Maybe he fell." This went on for about a half hour. The Chief walked into the Detective Bureau and said, "Hey, who beat the shit out of Kurst? he looks like the elephant man!" I looked at Sgt. Smith, then the Chief, and said, "I did, Chief; he had it coming." The Chief looks at Smith and says, "Good Job, Gary. we don't put up with that around here," and walks out.

Sgt. Smith was furious, he snuck out and went to the holding cell area, and the dispatcher called us down to dispatch; we were watching Sgt. Smith on Camera interacting with Kurst. We couldn't see Kurst because he was in the cell, but we watched Smith hand him a piece of paper through the bars. It was an Internal Affairs complaint form; after about 15 seconds, we saw a crumpled piece of paper fly out of the cell and hit Smith right in the face. We all almost fell over; we were laughing so hard.

What a dirtbag, Sgt. Smith tried to get my suspect to file an Internal Affairs complaint against me.

As we were processing the evidence, A patrol officer took Mr. Kurst out of the holding cell so he could transport him to the County Jail. As Mr. Kurst passed by us, he stopped and said,

Kurst: "Detective Pacelli?

Me:" Yeah, what's up, Brad?

Kurst:" I had that coming; I was out of line; we're even, right?

Me: "Yeah, we're cool."

Kurst: "Tell Smith that I ain't no fuckin Rat."

Me: "You got it, Brad."

Nobody liked Sgt. Smith, but he was very persistent,

When I was a Detective in Wanaque, I dealt aggressively with the drug abuse problem in town; Sgt. Smith wanted nothing to do with drug cases. He didn't know anything about it, and instead of letting me do what I was hired to do, he always put obstacles in my way. I even went as far as telling Smith that he could have all my drug arrests. He could go before the town administrator and show him how great he was. That was all he cared about anyway, but he refused. He would rather hinder my progress. He was a small thinker, and I was always two steps ahead of him.

I squeezed our local heroin users so much that they would put disguises on to take the bus to Paterson to buy heroin. One day, we caught one of our regulars when he got off the bus after buying down in Paterson; he was dressed as a Hasidic Jew. He had the hat and the wig with the curls, the entire costume. I almost let him go; he put a lot of effort into his costume, but it didn't matter; they couldn't move without us knowing about it, I had a few good informants, and they always let me know what was happening.

Don't misunderstand me; I have compassion and empathy, but it's directed toward the real victims. These dirtbags were responsible for all the burglaries in town. We didn't have any master jewel thieves in town breaking into houses, and what lit a fire under my ass was when one of these scumbags broke into an older woman's home while she was at her husband's funeral of seventy years. That was a War Declaration, and if they wanted a fight, they would get one.

I was always in Paterson at the Sheriff's Department Headquarters, using my contacts and working with the County Detectives. All our drug buyers got their drugs in Paterson, so I believed hitting them at the source was the way to go; it would dry up their supply. While I was down there, I would always run into the Sheriff, and my old partner Jose and the Sheriff saw how aggressive I was.

Smith hated this and would always complain to the Chief. The Chief ignored him; I was doing exactly what the Chief wanted me to do.

I had been going back and forth with Jose about returning to work at the Sheriff's Dept., but nothing was official. I had it made in Wanaque, but Sgt. Smith was never going to stop, and he came from a political family; he was prominent in the church, as they always are. Smith would be Chief someday, whether I liked it or not.

I was qualifying with my weapon at the range when my phone rang, and I answered it,

Me: Detective Pacelli.

Caller: Gary, this is the Sheriff; Jose says you want to come back to the Sheriff's Department.

Me: Yeah, ok, you're the Sheriff; tell Jose I said to fuck off!

I hang the phone up. I didn't need Jose breaking my chops at that moment; I had a lot going on; I called up Jose and started yelling at him. Jose swore it was legit and was standing in the Sheriff's Office.

Oh, Boy, what did I do?

The Sherriff got back on the phone; I started to apologize, but he cut me off and he said:

Sheriff: "This is the Sheriff, Jerry, Jerry Speziale; Jose says that you want to come back to the Department,"

Me: "Yes, sir, I wou—" he cuts me off again.

Sheriff: "Narcotics, start tomorrow."

Me: "I have to give two weeks."

Sheriff: "Done, two weeks."

The Sheriff hung up; I called Jose, and Jose Said, "Welcome back, kid."

My head was spinning; I respected Chief Reno. He had always been good to me and had taken care of me, but he was starting to feel pressure from Sgt. Smith. It would only be a matter of time before Smith got me. This may be the best solution for all of us.

I went and saw Chief Reno. He knew everything that was going on with his most senior Sergeant. I asked him if he would sign my intergovernmental transfer; if he refused, I would have still gone, but I would not have had civil service protections.

Chief Reno agreed to sign my transfer; he knew it was the best way out of a hot situation, and in doing so, he gained the respect of the new Sheriff. It was a win for him. The Sheriff prioritized him when assigning officers to the newly formed Task Force. Sgt. Smith looked like the petty, small vindictive person that he was. I warned the Chief and told him that he thought Smith was his friend, but he would be the reason why he would get pushed out and into retirement. Sgt. Smith replaced him years later as Acting Chief, but he failed the Chief's test twice and was forced to retire also. In my opinion, Sgt. Smith was a coward; he refused to come to work on my last day, showing his true colors.

When I left the Wanaque PD, I was replaced by a good friend and a fantastic Detective, Detective Sahanas. Sahanas was aggressive and did a great job.

I reported to the Sheriff's Department two weeks later. I first saw the Warden. The Warden was just an officer the last time I worked there three years earlier; I knew him and his brother well. They grew up in Wanaque, and the Warden went to High School with my brother, and I went to High school with his brother, the Deputy Warden.

I walked into his office, and he said hello, and we laughed and joked for a few minutes until he said, so, how's it going in Wanaque? What brings you here?

I told him I was told to report to him today and that I worked there now.

The Warden looked at me and said he knew nothing about it and never received an order. My mind began to race. Could this happen? I showed him my transfer form. He looked at me and started to laugh; whew, that scared me for a minute. I thought you were serious. The Warden says, "I am serious. I don't know anything about it."

The Warden walked out of his office and made a phone call; he stepped back in, smiling; that was a good sign.

You're good, Gary

Ok, that's good; we discussed a few things, this administration was brand new, and everyone was still feeling their way around their new jobs. We discussed my pay and time off and all the essential things; it was the honeymoon period, and everybody was excellent; I got a substantial pay raise and an extra five vacation days.

No one knew where my narcotics office was. I called Jose and found out where to go, and he told me to hurry up so we could go out to lunch. I saw nothing had changed; I told him to go. I didn't want to hold them up. I headed over to the POD, that's what it's called when you're assigned to the DEA, and you work out of a satellite office; it's called a "Post of Duty" I was assigned to Group 9, stationed at the Paterson Post of Duty. I got to the office, which was hidden in a bank building. The FBI was across the hall, and the ATF was in the next bank building over.

Everyone was gone except for the Chief, Chief Tom Murray. The Chief let me in and asked who I was. I told him my name and that I now worked for him. He shook his head and said that Jose had mentioned something about it, but he never received anything official. He was glad to have me aboard, but since no one had given him the heads up, he didn't even have a car for me. He told me to ride along with Jose till he found me a car.

Chief "Tommy" Murray was the best supervisor I have ever worked for. He was a retired Lieutenant from the New York City Police Department. He worked with Jerry Speziale before he became Sheriff when they were both assigned to the DEA from the NYPD; these guys were the real deal. He would hang out with us whenever we went to a bar after work, and you were never allowed to call him "Chief" outside of work, a real supervisor. A leader, not an administrator; You just knew he had your back.

So, I rode with Jose till I got my car. It was just like the old days; we had a great time. We had fun laughing and eating, driving around, eating, making fun of each other, and eating. When we found time after eating, we even did some work. We hit a heroin mill on my third day there; we followed a vehicle from the Heroin mill to an apartment in Irvington, NJ; when the car left Irvington, we boxed them in at a red light. They had forty-six thousand dollars in a hidden trap. The trap was an inside compartment that opened and closed using hydraulics. We headed back to the apartment; when we got inside, the resident had taken off already.

We noticed all these bags filled with empty glassine envelopes used for packaging heroin. There were so many of them; we suddenly realized they weren't empty; they were full, eighteen-thousand bags of heroin. A heroin mill in the next town over, twelve kilos of heroin in one vehicle, and eight kilos of heroin in another. Not bad for my third day there; I knew I would like this job. I needed to pay attention and learn fast.

I finally was at a job where everyone was competent, no one was insecure in their positions, we worked hard, long hours, and we never complained; when we left our houses for work, we never knew when we would be home or where we would end up. There was no picking your kids up at the school bus stop or leaving to go to "soccer practice"; we worked the job and went wherever it took us. Sometimes it would be weeks before we would walk onto our headquarters. We always had a change of clothes and some toiletries in a bag in our cars, and we peed in water bottles when we had to. We all loved what we were doing, our bosses treated us well, and we respected them.

The Chief located an excellent undercover car a few days later; it was a newer Pontiac Grand Am, and I loved it. I felt like I was in that 80's show "Miami Vice,"

I didn't tell anyone I had left Wanaque; everyone outside my group thought I was on loan from Wanaque. I would see them at the motor pool when I was gassing up, and they would always ask me how it was going at Wanaque. Great, I would say. You cannot become a target of some supervisor on a power trip if you don't work there.

Chapter 6

They came with what I call the fishing net; since I could not move, they had to scoop me up with this tarp-like material and attach it to what looked like something you would use in a mechanics' garage. It looked like an engine lift. They would scoop you up, drop you on another bed, and off you would go. I remember thinking a few funny thoughts whenever I was in the "net."

I would imagine myself being in one of those arcade games, the one where you try to snatch the prize up with the mechanical claws. I would imagine myself behind the glass, or the other one was when you see them open the fishing net on the deck of a ship. All the fish come splashing out; I could envision myself falling out of that net with all the fish flopping around me. When you are in my situation, you must have a sense of humor, or you will lose your mind.

I got my room; it was nice but scary. I couldn't hit the nurse call button, and if they closed the door to your room, it was like you were on Mars, you were truly alone; they had a habit of closing the door; I know that doesn't seem like a big deal. So, imagine you're in a straight jacket, in a room with a closed door, in an empty house on a farm. That's what it felt like to me.

When I got to my room, The nurse went through the plastic bag that had my belongings; let's see what I had:

Pair of sneakers

Wallet

Phone (no charger)

Pair of socks cut down the sides

Underwear cut down the sides

Shorts, cut

T-shirt, cut

Wingsuit, shredded

That's it, no clothes, no toiletries, no anything.

The nurse searched around and found me a pair of sweatpants, a T-shirt, and some socks. She also found me a charger for my phone. Since I was paralyzed, I couldn't use the remote for the TV, so I asked her to leave it on a channel that played the show, "Forensic Files," back-to-back. I have seen every episode; I think I could qualify as a forensic expert in court if I had too now.

Since I couldn't hold or dial my phone, Kristin would have to call the nurse's station and see if someone was available to come into my room and call her back with my phone and lay it on my chest. Good times.

I refused to facetime Kristin; I did not want her to see me in my condition. I didn't want to worry her any more than she was. I was in bad shape; my hands were curled in at the wrists, and I hadn't showered or shaved for about twelve days. That's when Kristin got a hold of the head nurse and told on me, and boy was I in trouble, one of my favorite nurses came in and demanded that I facetime Kristin; of course, I refused, so she said, "I won't feed you."

I said, "Cool."

I really didn't have an appetite anyway, but then she pulled her Ace out of the deck, "I'll put a sign on your door, requiring that your door remains closed at all times," I lose, I cried "Uncle," immediately and then I began face-timing Kristin. You have to understand my point of view; I had been telling Kristin that I was good and would be OK and walk out of that Hospital. It's not that I didn't believe what I was saying, I didn't know how I was going to pull it off. I began Face-timing Kristin, which made us feel a lot better.

I asked Kristin to call two people for me, Lauren and Shauna, at Skydive Sussex. Skydive Sussex was my home drop zone, Lauren was the drop zone manager, and Shauna was the senior rigger, and she ran the rigging loft, they were both my friends, and I knew they would help me out and stay in touch with Kristin.

I decided to stay in North Carolina for my therapy, even though I missed my family. I knew that I had one chance to get it right, I needed to be disciplined, and I thought it would be easier on everyone if I stayed where I was. This was my only chance, whether I walked out of this Hospital or got wheeled out in a wheelchair was going to be up to me, and I wasn't going to blow it. Kristin agreed and understood my decision. She knew that when I put my mind to something, I put my heart into it also, I gave it everything I had, and I promised her that I was walking out of that Hospital, and I promised myself that I was going to skydive again.

Most people don't understand why it was so crucial for me to want to skydive again or how I could even consider it while I was in the shape that I was in. Some people will never understand that I needed to physically get back to where I was before my accident; I could not just stop Skydiving because I had an accident. That isn't who I am, and to tell you the truth, everyone with an opinion or a judgment about whether I skydive again can kiss my ass; I'm a grown man. If my wife is OK with it, it's no one else's business. I have lost friends and family over this; people can say the stupidest things at times; I mind my own business and don't judge anyone, I am humble,

45

and I don't think I'm better than anyone. I wish everyone would learn to do the same.

I jumped one cloudy day; the cloud cover was high, so we were able to jump, and it turned out to be one of, if not the most incredible, jump I ever did. As I said, it was cloudy, so I wasn't expecting much from this jump. I was at Skydive Sussex and once I exited the plane, it began to rain, which usually would be a bummer but not this day! The raindrops were falling at the same speed I was falling, and you could see the individual raindrops. Since they were going at the same speed as me, they looked like they were not falling and were suspended in the air.

I could ride the raindrops down! it looked like something out of the movie "The Matrix." This is the stuff that keeps me skydiving, and you get to see and experience things that most people couldn't even dream about.

Now what determined when I got transferred to the physical therapy wing of the Hospital had nothing to do with the amount of movement I had recovered. I had to ween myself off the intravenous narcotics they had me on, and they would transfer me.

At this point, I had no visible movement; I was being fed and bathed by the nurses, and I felt helpless and useless. My body was slowly turning itself back on, and the nerve pain was excruciating, but I couldn't get therapy every day, that I sat there in a morphine-induced bliss.

I had messed up; I let my family down, and I let everyone down. I let myself down, and I was going to make this right or die trying. There was no room for negotiation, so I started to think about the "voice." Both voices the positive and the negative. I began to think about everything that had happened, from when I got hurt when I was a Detective and my current situation, and I started to believe that there was more at work here than I could see and as it became more apparent, I got stronger. I went over everything that happened step by step:

- Had I listened to the voice, I would have never jumped and not gotten hurt.
- I didn't listen, I broke my neck, but it broke in a way that didn't sever my spinal cord.
- I met and jumped with the military guys the day before; they knew my plans and most likely saved me from being paralyzed
- I was able to make it back to the drop zone, using my head, saving valuable time and my life.
- The magical wind from nowhere turned me 180 degrees and put me in the backyard across the street from the DZ. Slowed me down and cleared the trees. This is all on my GoPro video!
- The wind turned me and allowed me to land into the wind, slowing me down.
- I hit the chain link fence, and it absorbed the impact. Saved me.
- The Medevac decided to take the longer trip to the better hospital.
- Against all odds, I had no broken bones or internal bleeding.
- Dr. Bagin is one of the best neurosurgeons on the east coast; he just happened to be in the Hospital that day.
- I was at one of the best physical therapy hospitals in the country.

You're probably thinking, OK; you got really lucky that day, very unlikely but possible.

I almost forgot the very loud command to "shoot him, Shoot him now!" And my partner showed up at the last possible moment and saved me from getting creamed by the tractor-trailer. That's twice that I escaped certain death by forces beyond my control, and there is a third time; later in the story, you will, no doubt, see that no one is that lucky.

I began to realize that no one is that lucky, and if God had a role in all of this, why would he do all these things so that I could be paralyzed and lay in a bed for the rest of my life? If that were true, something was wrong; I wouldn't wish that on my worst enemy; it would be beyond cruel.

No, if this were God's hand at work, I would take the whole ride out of this hell I was in. How could I not be optimistic? I know the ending. I do the work, I slip, I backslide, I'm human, but God picks me back up, shakes it off, and I work harder. That's the plan; I called the nurse in and asked if she could contact the Doctor and start weening me off the IV narcotics. Back to reality, time to pay the piper.

Let's get this going.

I was transferred to the physical training wing of the Hospital late on a Saturday night, and the transfer did not go well. When you are in a hospital, you must be your own advocate; you must speak up and sometimes fight for the proper treatment. I was learning fast that when you are paralyzed or disabled, people treat you differently. They don't see you. Your helplessness repulses them; they don't even realize it; I'm sure that before I mangled myself up, I was the same way.

Have you ever stopped to talk to a stranger in a wheelchair? Said Hello. How are you doing? You know, just like you would speak to any other human being that crossed your path. I never did; most people become very uncomfortable around disabled people. I'm not talking about someone who scammed a disability pension and gets a handicapped parking sign because they have "back pain." I'm talking about visibly disabled people. I now go out of my way when I see people in wheelchairs or walkers or prosthetic limbs to stop and talk; I want them to know that I see them, they are important, they matter, and you would be surprised; some of them have some fantastic stories.

My intake was a disaster, the physical therapy wing was in the same facility but was a different company, and I had to be accepted into the therapy program; they specialized in Spinal Cord Injuries (SCI); it was late on a Saturday night, the regular staff was off for the weekend, and the intake staff that was on, to be nice, English was their third language. They spent the next two hours trying to get me to sign the intake forms; I could not hold a pen, and they didn't believe me. They thought that I was lying or faking it. They wouldn't stop, they would put the pen in my hand, and it would fall out. I asked them to put the pen in my mouth, and I would try, but they refused. I asked them to call my wife, and she could sign for me, but they refused. I'm patient, but I flipped, I lost it, I told them where to stick the intake papers and demanded that they take me back to my room, it looked like I would be heading back to New York after all, and I didn't care, I got hurt, I didn't get stupid, and I wasn't going to take it anymore.

The nurses I had encountered up to this point were top-notch; ninety-nine percent were just the most incredible people I had ever met, the nurses' aides were fifty/fifty, the good ones were great, and the others were there for a paycheck. The hardest thing when you are a male and can't move in a hospital is getting a shave or your fingernails cut. The nurse's aides expect your family to take care of that for you; if you don't have any family, too bad. I get it, but I don't. Just as a human being, you can't go the extra mile and give another human being their dignity back by doing a simple thing like clipping a few fingernails or running an electric shaver over someone's face.

It's such a small thing, but it makes a huge difference for someone.

When I was on patrol, I never had the luxury of pulling up on a scene and saying, "that's not my job." I never shaved someone or cut their nails, but I'm not a nurse's aide, and no one calls the cops for a manicure.

I remember I got a call one night, that a woman was going into labor. No big deal, the ambulance was on the way; I was the first responder, so I walked into the kitchen of the apartment, and Holy shit, it looked like a chainsaw massacre. There was blood everywhere, I do mean EVERYWHERE! The woman was on the floor; she had given birth and was holding her baby, but her placenta never dropped. It was still attached to her but not to the baby, and the umbilical cord was spitting out blood like a lawn sprinkler. I walked over, but all that blood on the linoleum floor was slippery; I slipped, went down, and was covered in blood. I grabbed the woman's umbilical cord and squeezed it to stop the bleeding. There was no time to put my gloves on; it wouldn't have mattered anyway, with the blood I already had on me. I was squeezing the umbilical cord, and I felt her pulse through the cord. It was gross, but it was strong, and that was good. I had no choice.

My Seargent walked in, looked at me, covered in blood and holding the cord, and started laughing at me. I yelled at him to get something to clamp the umbilical cord off with.

The Sergeant reached into his pocket and handed me a paperclip. I told him to shove it up his ass and to get on the radio and roll the paramedics; this woman had lost a lot of blood. The volunteer ambulance Corps showed up and thank God they were prepared; I passed off the cord and walked out; everybody thought it was funny and had a good laugh. I had to shower and put a fresh uniform on, but my point is, I was a cop, not a paramedic or Doctor; I couldn't tell the women's husband to grab the cord and wait for the ambulance.

Once I was done flipping out and demanding to get sent back to my hospital room, they finally let me sign my papers with the pen in my mouth, and I settled in for a battle. I thought to myself, where the hell am I? I'm not taking any shit from anyone; no one is getting in my way! My guard was up, they gave me my meds, and I finally passed out.

I think if we just had a little compassion or empathy toward each other, the world would be a much better place.

This accident changed me, it took me some time to fully realize and appreciate the gift I had been given, and I was about to get an excruciating lesson on humility.

Chapter 7

I boarded the plane, and everyone was there, Sam, Rich, Logan, Katie, Corinne, and Dario. It was summer, so the door was open, and we got to altitude quickly; everyone was checking their gear, and we heard the customary yell from Dario.

"Have fun Motherfuckers; the first one to die is a rotten egg."

Everyone began to exit the plane; whoosh! Whoosh! Whoosh! Whoosh! I exit. My body hits the wind; I'm stable.

What the hell?

I'm not dropping down. I'm going up, and I can see the plane below me. It's getting smaller and smaller; what do I do? Do I deploy my canopy?

My eyes open, and I'm breathing fast. Where am I? oh man, I'm in a hospital, but this isn't my room.

Excuse me, sir,

Yes.

We have to catheterize you. It's been six hours since it was done last.

Oh, crap, I remember; I'm in the PT wing.

I had to be catheterized every six hours, which was probably the one thing I could feel; it was no joke, mainly because they wouldn't leave it in; they were worried about an infection.

Back to reality, I lay there, totally embarrassed, humiliated, and dejected. It is what it is. Suck it up, buttercup.

What were you thinking?

You got what you deserved!

It is Sunday morning, the first day of my journey.
How do you eat an elephant?
One bite at a time.
Pass the salt, please.
Let's Roll!

When Dario was working to become a Tandem Instructor, he had finished all his training and had to complete some actual tandem jumps with people. I volunteered. I trusted Dario's ability, he was an excellent Skydiver, and he was always willing to teach you or share knowledge, unlike some of the other "Skygods" that looked down on anyone who didn't have as many jumps as them. You always heard Dario before you saw him, and he was full of life; he reminded me of myself, thirty years younger, he was probably a little insane but no different than any of us, and I wasn't going to turn down a free jump.

He harnessed me up, and we got on the plane; I had done one tandem; it was the first jump I went on when I started my mission to get licensed. I didn't like it then and didn't think this time would be different. It was a control thing; when you go on a tandem after you are licensed, it's called a front ride. You surrender all control; when you're a student, you don't know any better, but once you're licensed, you know, there is no getting around it. You have zero control, and it's a little weird.

We exited the plane perfectly, the freefall went perfectly, then Dario deployed his canopy, and we went into a spinner; usually, when you open, you are looking at the horizon; when you're in a spinner, you see the ground. Dario maneuvers the toggles and slows the spin down; I look up, and we have some severe line twists.

I yell to Dario, "do you want me to do anything?"

Dario responds in the typical Dario way: "Yeah, shut the fuck up! And don't kick."

With all the formal training I have had throughout my life, the one thing that I am good at is following orders, most of the time.

I relaxed and settled in for the show; I was having one hell of an exciting front ride.

Dario began to kick in the opposite direction of the line twists, and he immediately stopped the spinning, but there were so many line twists that I wondered if he would get us out of them in time before we reached our decision altitude or hard deck. Your hard deck, or decision altitude, is a pre-determined altitude that a Skydiver determines. Suppose they reach that altitude and do not have a good, functioning canopy over their head. In that case, they immediately pull their cutaway handle on their harness and then immediately pull their reserve canopy handle: releasing the bad canopy and putting a good, functioning reserve canopy above them. The process happens extremely fast, and if you were just a tandem student on your first jump, you probably wouldn't even notice what happened. That's how fast and smooth the process can be.

Dario worked hard to get us out of the twists; he did it; I yelled to him, "We good?"

Dario: "We're good!"

We landed, we landed, and just sat in the field laughing; it's a great feeling when you are safe and on the ground. Dario has probably done hundreds of tandems since that day.

I had no idea I would experience that feeling of helplessness again under canopy, but that's what my accident felt like, a front ride. A front ride, but who was steering the canopy? It took me a long while to figure out and accept the reality of my situation that day and in life itself. We think we are alone during hard times, and when things are going well, we believe we have done it all ourselves. This way of thinking couldn't be any further from the truth; the truth is that God is our Tandem Instructor, he lets us play with the toggles, and we believe we are steering our canopy or our life, but when things go bad, God is there to take control if you want him to.

Sunday Morning, breakfast at 5:30, dressed in the only attire I had, Sweatpants, a t-shirt from the "lost and found," hospital socks, and my diaper, yes, my diaper. I was in control of my bowels, but they weren't taking any chances, and I didn't have any underwear. Big Lenny would be bringing me all my clothes and personal items from the hotel room soon, and the plan was that Kristin would come down when I thought it was a good time. Visit me and take whatever I didn't need home.

I did not want Kristin to visit until I at least was able to transfer myself from my bed to my wheelchair, and that was a long time away. I also did not want to be in a diaper. Lenny would be coming soon, I needed clothes and my laptop, but I foremost needed Lenny. There was no way that I would be able to use a computer; I couldn't even manage my iPhone. I needed Lenny to get into my laptop and retrieve my passwords for Kristin so we could pay our bills that were starting to pile up. When you get hurt and are down for the count, the world does not care. There are no timeouts. Thank God Lenny was four hours away and such a good friend.

Speaking of diapers, looking at myself in this giant Diaper was humiliating, but it reminded me of when I was a Detective in Wanaque. I was sitting home one night, hanging out with Kristin, when I got a call from the on-duty Sergeant at the Wanaque PD. He asked me to come into headquarters. I asked him what he had and why he was calling me. I wasn't on call.

The Sgt. explained that he had called Sgt. Smith, and upon explaining what he had, Sgt. Smith refused to come in and hung up on him. I asked the Sergeant if the on-call Detective Sergeant wouldn't come in, why should I come in when he wouldn't even explain what he had. The Sgt. said he didn't know what he had but knew it wasn't something he should be handling.

Fair enough, I told the Sergeant that I would be there in ten minutes.

When I got to headquarters, the Sergeant met me in the parking lot and said he wanted to brief me. I didn't understand why I needed to be briefed outside, so we went into the building, and I suddenly understood everything. I understood why Smith refused to come in and hung up; I understood why the Sergeant wouldn't tell me what he had and wanted to brief me outside.

I walked in, and in the corner of the squad room, standing on a plastic tarp, was a 6'4," three-hundred-pound naked man wearing a soiled diaper with feces running down his leg. The smell was unbearable, and the worst part was the smug, arrogant look on this freak's face.

The Sergeant explained that the "Diaper man" was stopped by one of the patrolmen after he kept driving through the Burger King drive-through, and they called the Police; apparently, the Diaper man had a dirty diaper drive-through masturbation fetish.

Let me say that again. The Diaper Man had a dirty diaper drive-through masturbation fetish!

The teenage girl working the drive-through became terrified that this naked giant in a diaper kept repeatedly ordering an inexpensive item and driving through the drive-through so he could see her.

I know it's not acceptable in today's world, but this was around the year 2001; things were much different, and my initial reaction was to beat the living shit out of this weirdo, no pun intended. Thankfully he smelled so bad, and I didn't want to get any on me.

I asked the Sergeant why he didn't charge him and send him to the county jail. The Sergeant says, "that's the kicker; I can't find any laws that Diaper man has broken!"

We stayed there all night trying to figure out what to charge Diaper man with; he hadn't exposed himself and didn't threaten or harass anyone. All he did was crap himself and order five sodas, one at a time. The Patrolman refused to put him in the back of his vehicle, and he made Diaper man drive himself in his own car to the Police Department Headquarters while he followed behind him.

The diaper man knew the game. He admitted that he was on probation from a charge he received in the next county over; he showed up in the County courthouse in his soiled diaper and refused to leave, they charged him, and he was on probation. I stayed there all night; I couldn't put Diaper man in the cell. He wasn't under arrest; I had to sit there and babysit this giant nutcase all night. He was on probation, so I figured I would call his probation officer first thing in the morning and see if they could violate his probation. This dude needed to be off the streets, but the thing is, Diaper man, cooperated just enough. He was polite, smug, and arrogant, but he didn't commit a crime, we couldn't charge him, and the Diaper man was enjoying watching me sit there repulsed and enraged by him.

I finally got his probation Officer on the phone, and we talked for about an hour. There was nothing we could do; probation couldn't violate him. I reached out to the Passaic County Prosecutors' office and got an assistant Prosecutor on the phone, and we wracked our brains trying to find something to charge him with, but nothing. I had to let him go. I couldn't believe it. Out the door, he went, but I wasn't done. I started calling every town in Northern New Jersey, asking for any reports they had on the Diaper man. By three in the afternoon, I had a two-inch file on this maniac. I had over fifty-six incidents like what just happened.

I called his probation officer and asked him if he knew of the fifty-six incidents involving the Diaper man. To my shock and horror, his probation officer had all those reports and still could not violate him. Unbelievable, that confirmed that my initial instincts were correct; I vowed that the next time I encountered the Diaper man, I would beat the hell out of him. I would dress appropriately, but this would not solve the problem; it would stop the Diaper Man from ever returning to Wanaque, and he would move on to another town. That would be the best solution I could offer the hard-working residents of the Borough of Wanaque! I was employed precisely to protect them from people exactly like Diaper Man! Amazing. I understand mental illness, but this creep was not mentally ill. He was just a perverted giant freak; he was a predator.

The Nurse came into my room and explained that they had an opening in physical therapy and that I could go if we hurried. I was like, "yeah, I'm ready for that; let's do it." We would have to hurry, and I hadn't ever been put into a wheelchair yet, and I needed to be catheterized. The Nurse got three other people to help transfer me into the chair. It was hard, they put a walker in front of me, and I couldn't even keep my arms on it; I was total dead weight, which was not very encouraging but a first step, nonetheless. They raised the back of the bed, and they swung my legs over the side, and they lifted, and I tried with every ounce of energy that I had to help. I can't say it was useless because it was the first time since my accident that my brain sent signals to the appropriate muscles, and that signal just had to find a path around the bruised, swollen section of my spinal cord, no small task.

Whew! I made it and was in the chair; this was good.

But

We forgot to catheterize me.

We had ten minutes to get there, or I lose the slot. This place was in high demand, and these training slots were precious.

The place was so outstanding that it had its own hotel located inside the hospital, which was extremely convenient.

The Nurse came in with the catheter and was rushing; I was getting a little nervous. She pulled my sweats down, grabbed my "thing," and shoved this two-foot-long catheter in me. Oh boy. That hurt. I felt something pop; she finished up, gave me my pain pills, and sent me on my merry way.

I want to try and explain what I felt like; I said that I was paralyzed and couldn't feel anything, which was accurate. I was numb all over, inside and outside. I could not feel anything with my hands, you could stab me with a knife, and I wouldn't feel it; my insides were numb, and it felt like there was a very tight belt around my mid-section, no pain but pressure. But if you could imagine being set on fire and suddenly frozen solid, and the fire was still raging inside. That is how I felt; the nerve medicine and the pain medicine helped, but it was something that you just had to get used to. I had mentioned that my body was slowly returning to life, and the pain was a good sign.

I got to therapy, and I met the therapist. I was the only one there, they were done for the day, but they wanted to evaluate me so they could get a head start for the following Monday. The therapist explained that training was Monday through Friday and on weekends on a first-come, first-served basis, and it had to be approved by your lead therapist. The typical day consisted of ninety minutes of physical therapy, ninety minutes of occupational therapy, and sixty minutes of recreational therapy.

He explained that a team would be assigned to me consisting of a daily physician, a physician assistant, a neurosurgeon, a neuropsychologist, a case manager, a lead physical therapist, a lead occupational therapist, a lead recreational therapist, a speech therapist, and a dietitian. They would meet every Thursday afternoon to review my progress and plan for the following week. Kristin would receive an email containing the progress report, the agenda for the next week, and a phone call from the case manager the next day.

This is where I needed to be; no wonder there was a waiting list to get into the program. It hit me hard how lucky I was, and I was grateful.

I must stop saying that! I need to say how blessed I am for being taken there.

The therapist then called their therapy gym on the floor below and asked for assistance to get me on the therapy table so he could evaluate me.

On the table, he asked me to try and move my body with his help, and I realized I could make minor movements of my large muscle groups. For example, I could move my right or left upper torso by using momentum and my trap muscles in my neck and could raise my legs individually or together about an inch off the table if I threw a kick. We were both impressed. They put me back in the chair, and he showed me this hanging harness on a track wrapped around the therapy ceiling. I told him that I was familiar with hanging harnesses and that we use something similar in skydiving training. He asked me if I wanted to give it a try.

Yes, sir, absolutely.

I didn't know it then, but they were testing me to see my motivation level; mine was off the charts.

They wheeled my chair to the harness and started to strap me in. I was terrified and afraid to see how bad I was. I kept holding on to having this sudden return of all my muscle functions, you know, "like a stinger,"

"No, it isn't." What a dick. Ha-ha!

Here we go. This harness was just like the fishing net. It slowly raised me out of the chair, and they gave me a walker, but I couldn't hold on to it. I tried so hard. I told the therapist how good it felt, for the first time in twelve days, to be looking at things from the level of if I were standing; I had been in bed for twelve days. I told him that I wanted to try and swing my legs so I could make believe that I was walking, and he said, "go for it" I swung my legs with every ounce of energy I could muster. I didn't care what it looked like, I was walking out of that hospital, and this was the journey's first step. I got about ten feet and had to stop. I was exhausted but completely satisfied, progress had been made, and I had taken the first bite of the elephant. It tasted horrible, but I knew in time I would first grow to tolerate it, then grow to like it, then love it.

He put me back into the chair and told me he knew I would be OK If I stayed positive and worked hard. He then asked me a question.

Do you know that your sweatpants are covered in dried blood?

No, what do you mean?

I looked down, and there it was. I had major neck surgery twelve days earlier, so I had a limited range of motion in my neck. The therapist lowered my sweatpants, and my diaper was also covered in dried blood. I had been bleeding a lot from my catheterization. I was concerned, not mad, not yet. Concerned. He wheeled me back to my room and told my Nurse.

When the therapist left, the Nurse told me it wasn't blood; it was Betadine. I told her I wasn't blaming anyone and wanted to see a doctor to ensure I was OK. She said no, because it was just Betadine, and I had nothing to worry about. I told her that I wanted to see the charging nurse immediately. She left and came back with the charging nurse. The charging nurse is the Nurse in charge of that shift; she walked into my room. She didn't tell me her name and began to tell me that it was not blood and that the therapist needed to mind his own business and not tell them how to do their jobs.

That was it. I lost it. I told both Nurses that I was retired from Law Enforcement and had twelve operations up to this point. I damn sure knew the difference between Betadine and blood, and if I didn't see the doctor on duty within the next hour, I was going to lodge a formal complaint against the two of them, and I finished off with:

"Now get out of my room, and don't come back unless you're with a goddamn doctor!"

Here I was. I had just made fantastic progress and had to be brought down to the pit of negativity because two "nurses" cared more about not admitting that they made a simple, forgivable mistake. They would rather me maybe have permanent damage. I'm in a hospital, not a mall; there are doctors here for this reason. I don't think I was being unreasonable.

Knock, Knock.

Come in,

In walks a doctor, my Nurse, and the charging nurse. I understand that the charging nurse is there to protect and cover for the Nurse, but I was not interested in blaming anyone. I just wanted to make sure my "stuff" was still in working order, I may be old, but I'm not dead. You know what I mean?

I told the doctor that the therapist noticed blood on my sweatpants and diaper, and I don't know how long it had been there, but I wanted to get it checked out to ensure everything was OK. I see the two nurses look at each other with relief. The doctor checked me out, saw a minor cut, and said I would be fine and that he would note my chart so the nurses would take extra care moving forward. That's all I was looking for. I'm not stupid. I was in a hospital, I had no family present, I couldn't move, there were ways that I could be made to suffer, and I wasn't up for the fight yet.

The shift ended, and the night shift came in; they put me back into my bed, and I realized how tired I was just from the little activity I had done. I wondered what tomorrow had in store for me, and I was nervous and excited. I took time to reflect on the small victories that I had just had, and I felt genuinely grateful. I was thankful for being alive. I'm grateful for not ditching it into the trees and not swallowing my tongue. I was going to be OK; I was going to walk out of that hospital, and I was going to skydive again; I didn't know how, but I knew that I would have help. God had done amazing things for me; I didn't know why but I knew that he would see me through it.

The next day I had the same Nurse, and she said with a heavy southern accent, "You gave it to me in a New York Minute. I told everyone not to mess with you," I said, "tell them all, I will give it to them in a New York second if I have to. I'm in bad enough shape; I'm not going to tolerate getting hurt needlessly." That Nurse turned out to be one of my favorites, and we got along great after that.

I began therapy, and the next day, I met my lead therapists and case manager, who were all great people. They explained how everything would work, and we wasted no time. We started on the table with them stretching me out. My body was locked in fight mode and tensed up, trying to protect itself. The first few days were exhausting. I would pass out in bed at 6:00 pm, wake up at 3:00 am, and feel electrical charges running down my toes and fingers. It was intense, but I figured that my body was healing itself. My lead physical therapist pushed me to the point of almost passing out. And I would tell her every morning to torture me, to make me suffer; she loved it, and at night she thought of new ways to push (torture) me. I figured that I had limited time with these incredible people. I wanted to make it count.

Chapter 8

When I left for recruit training, at the Marine Corps Recruit Depot (MCRD), on Parris Island, South Carolina, I loved saying all that; boot camp, I got into a big fight with my father the weekend before I left; he said he didn't think I had it in me and didn't want me to embarrass him. That burned a hole in my soul, and I vowed that the only way I was leaving that island was either a Marine or dead. That argument stuck with me till this very day; When I went to the Corrections Officer Academy, I won four out of five awards; I won the physical fitness, range-high shooter, academic, and distinguished graduate awards; I was also a Squad Leader and the Class Vice President. You should have seen the look on his face at my graduation; it was priceless. I still hold the record for earning the most awards.

If you truly put the work in and give it everything that you have, you can accomplish amazing things, but as I have said, we battle with our minds. Your mind can launch you to greatness or keep you down and afraid, afraid to fail; it can be your worst enemy.

My therapists and case manager were incredible people. They cared; they cared every day, not just sometimes. They encouraged me to set high goals and stay positive. They were amazed at my skydiving stories and convinced me I could go as far as I wanted, and the only thing holding me back was my mind.

I didn't get permission to use their names; otherwise, I would have. I wish they could get recognized for what they did for me. They were never negative; they cared and went above and beyond every day; they gave me hope and taught me how to live again.

My case manager was the best; she was accommodating, keeping Kristin in the loop and checking in on me. She came into my room that first week, asked me about my goals, and wrote them on my wall on this big whiteboard. On the top line, she wrote, I fell out of an airplane! She said that whenever I had a bad day or got discouraged, I was to read that and realize that I wasn't even supposed to be Alive! Whatever I was stressing about was nothing, and she said, just read that and realize how lucky you are.

The board looked like this:

I fell out of an airplane.
  I will pee on my own.
  I will walk out of this hospital.
  Those were my goals, straightforward, and I like to keep it simple.

The first week went uneventfully. I tried to get on the list for therapy that weekend but was denied; the therapist wanted me to rest. It worked out well, too, because Lenny showed up with my badly needed clothes and laptop. He set up my laptop and had me try to move the mouse or type; I couldn't do it. Lenny got into all my accounts and paid my bills; this would buy me time enough for when Kristin came down to visit, she could take the laptop with her and manage all the accounts. We were unprepared for this, I paid all the bills, and everything was stored in my laptop; nobody ever thought anything terrible would happen to them. We now have everything written down in a book like it should have been.

Lenny also dropped off my portable Blue Tooth speaker, and from that moment till I was discharged, my music was never off while I was in that room. It got to the point that some of the nurses and staff would come into my room and hang out because they liked my music. It got me through it; I would get back from therapy and listen to music till I left the room again, Classic Rock, 80's, 90's, and Country non-stop.

Sunday morning, I was lying in bed, staring at the bathroom door, deep inside my head, doing battle, when the housekeeping woman knocked and asked if it was OK if she cleaned the room. I told her sure, and honestly, I could use the company; weekends were rough there. I couldn't move, so I had two choices, lay in bed and stare at the bathroom door or have them put me in the chair and stare at the bathroom door; I had a window, but since I couldn't get around, the angle of view that I had was a brick wall. I later discovered that I had a view of a beautiful courtyard from a different angle, but that wasn't until the week before I left.

The housekeeping woman entered my room and closed the door; I thought that was strange because that hadn't happened before. She approached my bed and said:

Housekeeping: Excuse me, sir, can I ask you a question?

This is going to be interesting, I thought to myself.

Me: Sure.

Housekeeping: Are you that famous actor in all those car movies?

I started laughing.

Me: Do you mean Vin Diesel?

Housekeeping: Yes! That's you?

Me: No, I'm not Vin Diesel.

Housekeeping: I really want an autograph. Are you sure? Are you telling me the truth? Everyone downstairs thinks you're him!

I apologized that I wasn't him and told her if she came back in a few weeks when I could write, I would be happy to give her an autograph. She never really believed me; whenever she was assigned to clean my room, she always asked me, and it made my day every time she did.

I was starting to progress, and it was coming fast; I woke up every morning at 3 am and concentrated, beginning from my toes and working my way up to my head, contracting every muscle I could. I was retraining my brain to reconnect with my muscles. I started doing it to whatever song was playing. I just had to keep moving and getting stronger.

One day, I went to therapy, and when they brought me back to my room for lunch, I asked the Nurse to dial Kristin's number. Kristin answered the phone, and I could tell something was wrong. She said everything was fine, but after thirty-three years, you know when something is wrong. I could tell she had been crying, I asked her again what was wrong, and she began to cry and said that one of our dogs, Gunner, had died. I was speechless. Gunner was the coolest Golden Retriever ever; she was born on April 1, 2008. We were under Covid rules in New York and New Jersey, and Kristin was teaching from home using Zoom and had paused for lunch; Gunner walked into the room, laid down at her feet, and died. I couldn't believe it, I started to feel like my family and I were under attack. I had to get off the phone. I felt like such a piece of shit, stuck in that hospital, inside a body that I destroyed; I felt responsible and helpless to do anything about it.

I sat in my wheelchair, staring at the wall, wanting to throw in the towel, pack it in, and give up. I considered telling Kristin to put me in a nursing home and make believe I was dead; I closed my eyes and prayed. I asked for the strength to get back up, shake it off and carry on.

I started to remember all those Police Academy recruits I trained; there must be hundreds of them. I would push them to this place that I was in now. I was a great Drill Instructor. I'm not being conceited. My partner at the academy was even better than me. We worked as a team, and when we got on your ass, you were in deep trouble and couldn't shake us. We took no pleasure in our job, but it was necessary. We were the last line of defense; we had to weed out the recruits that slipped through the cracks in the hiring process. If they got past us, they graduated; they were given a badge, a gun, and the authority to use deadly force. If they weren't physically and mentally tough, they could get themselves killed, or even worse, their partner or someone else that didn't deserve it.

What do you get when you give an asshole a badge and a gun?

You get an asshole with a badge and a gun! It's simple stuff.

I could bring recruits to the point of total despair; one more nudge and most would have quit; then you make them, you make them find that tiny little flame inside themselves. However, it is that they find it; it usually requires them to acquire a deep hatred for you. It's a small price to pay, considering what's on the line. I wasn't there for them to like me. I was there to show them how to find the will to reach deep inside and survive. When they think that they can't take it anymore, they can. When they believe they will die if they do one more pushup, they won't. When they're getting their teeth knocked in, and they're about to die in some piss-smelling back alley, and they're about to give up, but they don't; they swallow the blood and the teeth, and they get mad, and they fight, and they fight like their life depends on it because it does. At that moment, they realize they're going to live, and they don't hate me so much anymore.

That's what I thought about, and I got mad, mad enough to go back to therapy and try harder and ask for more pain and suffering because the quicker I take the pain and put the work in, I can go home, not in a chair but on my feet.

I was making significant progress, they were putting me through hell, and I couldn't get enough of it; they were going all out for me. I was motivated, and I would give 100% every time they asked me to do something, just like when I was in boot camp or the police academy; every pushup they made me do only made me stronger, and the same thing happened in therapy. I had a great, positive attitude, and the other therapists noticed, and they said that I was extremely trainable; they only had to show me how they wanted something done once, and I would get it. Whenever a patient canceled, they came to me and asked if I wanted to fill the slot; I always said yes, and by the time I left, I was doing up to five hours of therapy a day.

The way it worked in this hospital was that the day shift nurses were responsible for everything. All your meals were had during the day shift, and all the patients were dressed and at their therapy appointments on time. And the beds were made, rooms cleaned, and the patients returned they were dressed and ready for bed. Nightshift was different. Not a lot going on. I had been in the hospital for eighteen days and had not had a shower yet; my skin was so dry it was falling off like dandruff.

I needed a shower. As I said, I would wake up at 3 am and do my little workout in bed. I had just begun to be able to hit the nurse call button, so I called the Nurse in and asked if I could be given a shower. I told her I hadn't had one since I had been there. She lied and told me it had to be done on the day shift because they were too busy. I knew she was lying; the

Nurse's station was right outside my door, and most of the time, they would sit there all night and laugh and joke; they weren't busy. So, I asked her if she liked to shower before she came to work, and she said that she did; I told her that since therapy was my job, why am I any different? Am I not a human being? Why can't I start my day feeling clean? She didn't answer; she just disappeared. I went to therapy feeling dirty and nasty, but I asked my therapist a question.

Realistically, how often should I expect to be given a shower? She told me around three times a week. She asked me why? I told her I hadn't had a shower since the day I had my accident, eighteen days earlier. I shook my head, and it looked like it was snowing; all the dead skin fell off me.

My therapist got up and made a phone call, and five minutes later, I was off to the side, talking to my case manager. She explained that eighteen days is totally unacceptable, we looked around at all the people in therapy, and most were old people, frail. Some with spinal cord injuries like mine were way worse off than me; some had given up, and some could barely speak.

She asked me if I wanted to file a formal complaint. I'm not a coward, but I was alone and had already seen what they could do to you if you got on their bad side, especially on weekends when there were no bosses around. I'd been left with my door closed for hours when I couldn't push the call button, and a few times since I had been able to press it, I've been locked in my chair, and the nurse call button had been hidden or put so far away from me that I couldn't reach it. I told her I wanted to shower, not go to war; she asked, what about all the other people who aren't as strong as me? What do you think is happening to them?

She was right. I had to speak out, wasn't I trained to defend the people that couldn't defend themselves? But I couldn't even protect myself. What hell would rain down on me?

I made the complaint, and the shit hit the fan, but it was so worth it; from that day on, I got showered every day at four in the morning, without fail; it's not like it was a big deal. I had a shower in my room. And I could do most of it myself, and I was getting stronger every day. They just had to help me get in my chair and onto the bench in the shower and bring me some towels. Not the end of the world. But a few nurses were super pissed; they didn't come after me. They went after my case manager and accused her of not having their backs. She was tough; she told them they were right, she didn't have their backs, and she was there to protect the patients if they weren't doing their jobs. What an incredible person. I was lucky to have her on my side.

A few days later, I was woken up around two in the morning by a nurse I had never seen. She was talking to another nurse, and they were standing over my bed on each side, talking as if I wasn't there. I interrupted her and asked her who she was; she told me her name and began talking again. I interrupted her again and said who is that? She told me it was her trainee. I asked what they were doing in my room, and she said she was training this Nurse to catheterize patients, and they were here to catheterize me. I said I wasn't due to be catheterized for four more hours, and she said, it's OK, don't worry about it. I told her you're not touching me until you get my Nurse.

She returned with my Nurse, and I then asked her if she was insane; she didn't understand the question, so I explained slowly. You come in my room, you don't introduce yourself, you begin to remove my blankets, you don't check my chart to see when I'm due for a cath, you don't ask permission, and you think it's OK to have a nursing student stick a two-foot tube up my penis. I'm not a training dummy; I'm a human being. You're lucky I don't have you arrested for assault, now get the hell out of my room, and don't come back.

I never saw them again.

From that day on, whenever there was a new shift and a nurse that I didn't know, I would not speak to them, take my meds, or cooperate in any way until they wrote their name and the Nurse's aide's name on the whiteboard as per policy. When they asked why, I politely explained to them, so I know your name when I file a complaint against you if you treat me like shit.

Don't get me wrong, this hospital was phenomenal, and most nurses were the most outstanding people I had ever met. Could you imagine what goes on in a bad hospital?

Things settled down after that, I had gotten a reputation as someone that wasn't going to play or be intimidated, and the nasty nurses and nurses' aides refused to work my room. We all got what we wanted.

Therapy was going great, but I always felt like I was running out of time. I was four weeks in, and I wasn't walking. I could stand for a little while, a very little while, but I didn't think I was strong enough to walk; I had zero feeling in my hand and was struggling with 2.5 lb. weights. Since I had no feeling in my hands, I dropped whatever I was holding if I wasn't looking at it. I had to retrain my body to do everything. I could barely brush my teeth, and I had to learn how to do everything left-handed because my right hand and side had way more nerve damage than my left side; I couldn't dress, I couldn't undress, forget about putting on socks or shoes, I still couldn't work my iPhone. The only way that I could eat was if they taped a spoon to my hand, and I used it like a shovel. That was a sight to see!

I was making progress with significant movements, like raising myself up from my chair or bed, swinging my legs off the side of my bed and sitting up, also transferring myself from the bed to the wheelchair and back, which was huge. I looked around the therapy gym, and I saw a lot of people with no hope.

They had given up, and I was really sad for them. I wanted to wake them up and somehow give them the hope that I had. I began to realize that I was blessed and had lessons to be learned and shared.

I was sitting in my wheelchair one day, and I asked my therapist a question: What would happen if you told me to get up and walk to the table?

She replied: I don't know. Get up and walk to the table.

Really? Really!

I slowly get up; I'm standing there without a walker, looking at the table ten feet away. It could have been a mile. Now or never, one step, another, my legs weighed 100 lbs. each, another step, two more, and I'm there, step, step. I grabbed the table. I made it; I walked. The whole place was clapping; I couldn't believe I had done it. Up to this point, the best I could hope for was being strapped to the walker because I didn't have the hand strength to hold on to it, a person walking behind me rolling my wheelchair in case I fell backward, and a person in front of me in case I fell forward.

I improved after that; it was the turning point. I still had so much work to do, but I knew I could do it. I walked a little more that day and they filmed it for me. I sent the video to Kristin, and she decided to come to see me; it was time. It didn't matter what I thought, I couldn't stop her if I wanted to, and I didn't want to... They were about to start putting me into the EXO-Skeleton suit. The suit would help retrain my brain to connect with my leg muscles, and they would be able to control my output level. The suit could totally walk for me, or I could do all the walking, and they could set it anywhere between. I was excited, and things were starting to go my way.

The day that I could take off my man diaper and put on my good "ole Haines" boxers was a momentous occasion, the irrational fear that I would have to wear diapers the rest of my life was terrible, but again this is what your mind does if you let it. I began working on my mind and learned to take control of my thoughts; when you spend a long time in a hospital, you begin to forget the little things you had enjoyed in your previous life; I was becoming institutionalized. Oh, what I wouldn't give for a nice hot cup of coffee, and then one day, this excellent Nurse came in and asked, would you like a cup of coffee? Say what? For real? She went and made me a nice big cup.

I had to drink it through a straw; I didn't care. I felt like a normal person again for a moment. The little things are so important. As I explained, after everything settled down after I lodged a complaint, the bad staff stayed away, and the staff I encountered were top-notch, and I was starting to get the same nurses and aides consistently. I formed some great friendships, and I will never forget how they gave me my life back, and I was learning to appreciate the little things we take for granted. Like a cup of coffee or wearing underwear and taking a shower!

Around the four-week mark, a few things started happening; as my nerves began to get turned back on, the incredible pain came. I was still on a massive dose of pain and nerve meds; it was a catch-22, If I lowered the number of pain meds, I would never be able to keep up with the therapy, so it was decided that the dose would remain the same. I began to have spasticity. Spasticity is extreme muscle spasms. I would have these when I woke up; the spasms were so intense that they resembled a seizure, and sometimes they were so intense it felt like my wrists would break. I began having lucid dreams. There was nothing special about the dreams other than that when I woke up, I would not remember that I was hurt and would think I was home in my bed. The worst thing about that was when reality hit me; it was always a significant letdown.

Back at home, things were tough on Kristin, I had been retired for quite a few years, and I would spend my time going to the gym and doing all the housework. I handled all the bills, laundry, grocery shopping, cooking, and cleaning. Nobody made me do anything, I did it because I enjoyed doing it, and honestly, I felt a little guilty watching Kristin get up at five every morning and head off to work. Don't misunderstand; Kristin loved her job as much as I loved mine, but I had it where all she had to do was go to work, and I had the rest. I loved my routine; the kids would get off the school bus and walk through the door, and I would be there with my apron on, cooking something for them. I know now that I wasn't helping them; I was hurting them, they had become too dependent on me, and now their worlds were turned upside down.

The neighbors were great. One of our neighbors that we are close with really went above and beyond; the day Gunner died, her husband came over and wrapped her in a blanket, took her to the veterinarian, and had her cremated; she is such a good friend that she wouldn't let us repay her. I will never be able to thank her enough. The other neighbors started a sign-up sheet and pitched in and rotated cooking meals for my family while I was in the hospital. Kristin was still working at this time, and it helped her stay focused; they were excellent, and I'm not that warm and fuzzy guy, but I hope they know how much I appreciate them.

I was improving fast now, and the doctors were impressed with my progress; this was the first time I was told I needed to write my story down; it could help somebody in a similar situation. I understood, but I had never written a book before. Where do you start? At the beginning.

The big day was coming up when I would see my wife for the first time since my accident; she was heading down with my sister-in-law, Lisa. Lisa is great, and she was a huge help through this nightmare. It worked out perfectly; Kristin needed to be trained before I could get released; she needed to be taught how to take care of me at home. I didn't think she would have to take care of me, but they weren't taking any chances. They agreed to train her on this visit, and hopefully, the next time she came down, she could take me home.

I had just earned my Skydiving "A" license at the end of the 2019 season, I ended the season with thirty-seven jumps, and I was starting the new year by taking a canopy course at Skydive DeLand in Florida. I was there with Rich; Big Rich was a 6-foot solid, disabled Army combat veteran from the Bronx in New York City. He had been blown up three times while deployed to Iraq. He had experienced similar injuries as me; he had (TBI), Traumatic Brain Injury and spent a significant amount of time unable to walk in a wheelchair.

I met Rich while completing my license course at "The Ranch" in Gardiner, New York. The Ranch was a large skydive center in Upstate New York and had a reputation as an "anything goes" drop Zone.

Rich and I had a lot in common; he was also prior law enforcement, we were the same age and had about the same amount of jump experience, and we immediately got along.

Rich was watching me land on this one jump, and as I mentioned, I was new to jumping, and my landings weren't pretty, and this landing was going to be Ugly. I came in, flared too late, popped up, hit the ground, and bounced a few times. Rich did not think I would get up after that landing, but I slowly got to my knees, then on all fours, and eventually stood up.

I didn't think much of it; that was why I took the canopy course in the first place. Later that night, I was looking at my phone, and on my home screen, I had an alert from a driving app. called LIFE360. The alert read, "It appears that you have been in an accident. Please contact us as soon as possible and let us know if you need assistance." We laughed our asses off; I hit the ground so hard that my phone thought I was in a car accident. At least I know that the App. works!

Kristin arrived just in time to see me try out the Exoskeleton; it was some serious technology. They strap it on you while you are sitting in your wheelchair, then turn it on, and it stands you up; the first time I used it, they let it do the walking for me, which was terrific. I walked down the hallway; the theory behind the technology is that it retrains your brain to fire the correct muscles in the proper sequence to teach you how to walk again. The second time I used it, they lessened the help the suit would give me, and my muscles would have to kick in and make me walk. The suit took two therapists to operate, and I could only imagine how much it cost. That day I did over a thousand steps with the suit; when I was done, they unstrapped me and made me walk on my own; they were right behind me with a safety strap attached to me, but I was on my own, no walker, no chair behind me. And I walked down the hallway and through the therapy gym; it was fantastic. It worked; my brain was rewiring my leg muscles.

Kristin stayed a few days and then headed home. It was great to see her, but I was in the zone. I had work to do, and I was running out of time.

Chapter 9

Jose had been speaking to Lenny, and Lenny told him about my accident and that my truck was still down at Paraclete. Jose called Kristin and explained that he had just booked a flight to South Carolina, and he would stay at Lenny's house for a few days, and then Lenny would take him to Paraclete, grab my gear and drive my truck home to New York. Jose wouldn't let Kristin pay for his flight or even take any gas money.

After I got off the phone with Kristin, I began to think about how I met Jose. When I started working in the Passaic County Jail in Paterson, N.J. I was a twenty-two-year-old country boy from a tiny northern New Jersey town called Wanaque. Growing up, I would get off the school bus, run home, grab my .22 caliber rifle or my single-shot 20-gauge Savage with the rifled .22 barrel on top, and meet my friends in the woods till it started getting dark. It was a far cry from how Jose grew up in Paterson.

Paterson was the third largest city in New Jersey. The Passaic County jail was well known for being a hell hole run by a no-nonsense Sheriff, I had been a corrections officer for about two weeks, and I hadn't even gone to the academy yet.

That day I was assigned to work the first floor and help the seasoned officers get the inmates out of the holding cells and onto the vans for court. The court officers were driving the vans, and I honestly had no idea what was happening; things moved fast. The inmates would come out of the holding cell, place their hands on the wall, get patted down, shackled up, and put into the vans.

Out came the inmates, and the officer (Jose), ordered them to turn around and put their hands on the wall so the court officers could pat them down and shackle them up. All the inmates turned around and placed their hands on the wall, except for one big dude, he started talking smack to Jose, and the next thing I knew, they started throwing punches. The court officers backed away; I had no idea what was happening, but my instincts kicked in, and I jumped on top of the inmate and started throwing punches. The next thing I knew, the other receiving officers came out, and we were all fighting on the ground. Once the mayhem stopped, everything was under control, and all the inmates got to where they were going, Jose found me in the hallway; he said, "what's your name, man? "Gary, I just started working here." 'Jose says, "You're a crazy motherfucker. I like you, but you punched me in the side of my head!" I apologized, and we started laughing. I did tend to get carried away when I got going.

Jose has a twin brother named Lazaro, that also worked in the jail; they were almost impossible to tell apart. I loved watching them two go at it with each other. They are beyond brothers or best friends; I have never seen a bond so tight between two people.

We were inseparable for our whole careers; after I went to the corrections academy, we were assigned to Uniform Transportation as partners; we took the inmates all over the state, wherever they had to go. We worked that assignment together till we were sent to the Police Academy together, and we then were assigned to County Patrol. We both landed on the Motorcycle squad as partners until Jose was transferred to narcotics as a Detective, and I went to work for the Wanaque

PD. I stayed in Wanaque until I returned to the Passaic County Sheriff's Dept. as a Detective first grade assigned to the DEA.

We usually drove around alone in our undercover vehicles on surveillance, but when we weren't on surveillance, we rode three deep, Me, Lenny, and Jose. Jose went to college with Lenny at Montclair State before they became cops.

Jose was in Miami working on a case with a money laundering group called "Eldorado" when I had my shooting incident, and his wife, Daisey, stayed with Kristin while I was in the hospital.

When Jose dropped the truck off at my house, my son Chase was there, and he asked "Uncle Jose" if he had seen me. Jose told him that he hadn't seen me but that I was tough and not to worry. He knew I would be OK.

My truck was home, and my gear was thrown in the back. I asked Kristin to drop my gear off at Skydive Sussex and get it to Shauna Finley; Shauna was my rigger and friend. I knew my gear was in bad shape and would take time to get fixed; I didn't know how much time.

Soon after Kristin left the hospital, I was cleared to get out of bed alone. I could also shower alone if I notified the Nurse's station. This was during covid so I couldn't leave my room; it would have been great if I could have wheeled myself outside, especially on weekends. Weekends were brutal, and I was trapped in the room, but I did manage to get visitors. Details of my accident spread throughout the hospital, and I would get visited by a nurse that had jumped when she was in the Army, and she would stop by, and we would talk about skydiving. It helped the time go by.

During therapy, they were taking me on longer and longer walks. I knew I was walking out of that hospital, but I was nowhere near recovered; I still couldn't put my shoes on, and the feeling in my hands was terrible. I was still numb all over, and to be discharged from the hospital, I had to be able to get up from the ground. When your legs are numb, and you try to get up off the ground, you cannot feel your knees on the floor. It makes it almost impossible.

I returned from therapy one afternoon, and there was a box in my room with my name on it. I asked the Nurse to open it if she didn't mind, and to my horror, it was filled with portable catheters. My therapist came into the room and opened one up, and explained how to use it. I asked her where I kept it, and she explained, in my pocket. She told me about her friend who plays in a wheelchair basketball league. He keeps it right in his pocket, goes into the men's room, and uses it. My stomach dropped, and I felt sick, like someone punched me in the gut. It hit home. I needed to pee on my own.

The Nurse called the doctor in, and we discussed if there was anything else we could do. There wasn't. They said it could take time, and I might never be able to go on my own. I spent the rest of that day sitting, pushing, and waiting in my bathroom. The next day I did the same. Whenever I had time, I sat on the toilet, and the Nurse kept checking on me. They seemed to be invested in this with me; you could feel the anticipation in the air. Nothing.

I was getting the itch to go home, I was a little overconfident, I had mastered my small space in my room, and I didn't realize how big the world was. I spoke to my case manager and got the ball rolling; I was going home in one week, and I was excited but nervous. I had to urinate on my own. Tomorrow was Saturday, and I didn't have therapy; I would concentrate and try to urinate all weekend.

"Here I sit, broken-hearted, paid my dime but only farted."
—Author Unknown

As I sat there, that poem I heard as a kid repeatedly played in my head; I'm dating myself with that poem. That poem was from a time when there were public restrooms that you had to pay to use, it was even before my time, but the poem was still around when I was a kid. The lightbulb went on. It was like a bolt of lightning struck me right between my eyes. I spoke the poem out loud. Here I SIT, brokenhearted, and paid my dime but only farted. That's it!

"SIT!"

No, I had to stand up and let gravity work!

I stood up and turned around slowly; this had to work; please, GOD, make this work.

I closed my eyes. I pictured a waterfall, a fire hose, anything, everything. I stood there for a long time, but I knew this was my last hope; if this didn't work, I would never truly feel "normal," not that it mattered, I could still live my life, but it was just so important to me.

It starts with a few drips, a trickle, and a stream. It hurt, not bad, but it's raw from being catheterized so many times. I don't care; thank you, God! My bladder emptied. And the weight of the world was lifted off my shoulders. I didn't flush; I called the Nurse and showed her. I told her what had happened, and I swear it looked like she was tearing up. She immediately called the doctor, and he ordered me to be scanned to see if my bladder had emptied. He didn't want me to get an infection. They scanned me, and I was good, but I wasn't out of the woods yet. I needed to urinate every six hours; if I didn't, they would cath me. If I went, I needed to be scanned. If I didn't empty, I must get cathed. We had to do this till Monday 6 am. I'm OK with that; I'm OK.

Monday came, and I was out of the woods. How much sooner could I have urinated had I just stood up? Ah, who cares? It's over. I'm slowly learning to let the past go, but I'm human, and I still get hung up on things in the past that I can't change.

And then I began to laugh, I remembered another short rhyme that I knew as a kid that seemed relevant at that moment:

"No matter how I wiggle or dance, The last drop will always fall in my Pants"

—Author Unknown.

Age is just a number. I will always be a kid at heart. I always find humor in the weirdest situations.

I still have a week of therapy to go, and I'm starting to realize that all these people have helped me so much here and that I will most likely never see them again. It upsets me; these people didn't just do their jobs. They became emotionally invested in my success or failure. They truly are heroes.

Dr. Bagin stops into my room one morning, and I'm sprawled out on the couch in my room. I'm lounged out in a way that made me look like nothing was wrong with me. We talked for a little while; I told him I didn't even have a scar on my neck. We talked about my hands, how they would take the longest to heal, and that I needed to be patient. He believed that they would improve, and he told me how great it was to see the recovery that I was making and the speed at which it was happening. He thinks that I should write a book. If my book helped just one person, it would be worth it. I asked how I could write a book. I didn't know how it would end, I thanked him for everything, and he explained that I needed to see a neurosurgeon up north to periodically check the hardware he put in my neck. We talked about skydiving, and he explained that there was nothing I could do that would generate enough force to damage his hardware. I started to laugh and told him, I hoped so, Doc, but you don't know me that well.

Therapy: they take me on a long walk around the hospital, it tires my legs out, but I'm OK. I have so much work to do when I get home. They are concerned; they wanted me to modify my bathroom, shower, and stairs, but I have yet to do them. I only bought a chair for my shower; I'm good and will adapt or improve.

Kristin and my son Chase arrived on Thursday afternoon. I was leaving Friday morning, and my discharge papers were already completed. I am leaving the hospital, but I am not nearly recovered; I'm a mess, and my back and neck muscles still have not been released. I could walk, but I walked with a limp; I'm not sure if I walked like a Mummy or a Zombie, and I didn't care. I knew that I would work hard and improve.

Friday morning, my Independence Day or discharge day, the staff gave me an Independence Day shirt, and I hugged everyone goodbye. The Nurse's aide assigned to me for the last few weeks was preparing to walk out with me, but we had a new head nurse that day, and she said, "you can't walk out. It's our policy; you must get wheeled out." Everyone looked at her and had a good laugh, and I, wait for it,

I WALKED OUT OF THAT HOSPITAL!

Thank you, God!

The next thing I knew, we were heading north in the car. I was going home. Here are a few things I could not wait to do:

See my family

Pet, my dog

Sleep in my bed

Shower in my bathroom

Smell the grass growing

Make my coffee

Spend time with my wife

And go to war; I am going into battle. I will battle my disabilities one by one; I am different from when I drove to North Carolina eight weeks earlier. I am a little slower and a little weaker, but I am wiser. I have a long hard road ahead of me, but now I will have my wife, Kristin, by my side, and when I stumble and fall, she will pick me up. When I cannot take it anymore and feel like venting, she will calmly listen and remind me how blessed I am. I am blessed. I have an incredible wife, a great family, and real friends. I have all these things to fight for. I have God as my bodyguard, the only way I can lose is if I quit and give up. That will not happen. I know that this will require pain and suffering. I had a doctor in New York refuse to examine my foot when I was experiencing problems; he looked me in the eyes and, with an arrogance that I have never seen, said to me," Do you think that after an accident like you had, that you would be able to walk away without any residual effects? My answer is twofold, yes, I do, and it's not for you to decide. I would need to get used to ignorant people, regardless of their titles.

I knew many people were mad at me. They needed to get over themselves. I've been through too much to care about what anyone says, but I am human and sometimes let the haters get to me. I have now been almost killed twice, and I think I deserve some peace; what I couldn't know now was that I had another dance with the Reaper on my schedule, and this one will be nothing to laugh at.

None of them were.

We decided that we would drive the eleven hours home without getting a hotel, it was a dumb move, but I was impatient to get home. We stopped for gas, and I decided to use the restroom in the gas station, I immediately noticed that things in the real world move much faster than in the hospital, and I felt vulnerable. I felt like everyone was looking at me as I limped around the gas station, I went to buy a soda, and I could barely carry it. I returned to the truck and couldn't close the door or put the seatbelt on myself. This was going to be more complicated than I thought.

"What did you think was going to happen? You got what you deserved."

I won't reveal who said that to me, partly because I don't want to hurt someone needlessly and partly because many people feel this way but won't say it to my face.

When you are fifty-three years old, you are supposed to stay in the box they expect you to be in. At my age, I was supposed to be fat, out of shape, look half dead, spend every day on the weekend doing the same as everyone else my age, getting drunk, getting fat, and repeating the next weekend. Now, I have no problem showing up somewhere after a day of doing something that I love doing, something that I have trained to do. That's not allowed; you have to stay in your box; see, if you get out of your box, you make everyone look bad. They don't want to have to look at themselves. What would they see? They would see unhappy people in unhappy marriages acting like they are having fun with other unhappy people doing the same thing. Stay in your box!

How about this idea? You do you, and I will do me; I won't judge you, and you don't judge me. That would be great.

I will be home soon; my dog is waiting for me.

My dog thinks I'm cool.

I thought about what had happened to me as I watched the headlights going south on Route 81. My life has been changed forever; I hoped that I could live a life worthy of the gifts that I had been given. I didn't know if I had been allowed to survive because I had a specific task to perform. I have been given ten lifetimes of spiritual understanding in five and a half minutes. Spiritual might not be the right word. I know I have been given a chance to face my death and come to terms with it. I have been able to be completely paralyzed and recover from it. That alone has shown me how precious life is and how every breath is a gift. Every day I can put my two feet on the floor and get out of bed is another chance to justify my existence and to treat all people with respect and dignity. I have a second chance at life. My slate is clean. I don't have to be dragged down by my past. It's gone. I'm free!

We cannot change the past, but the past can change your future, it can drag you down like an anchor, or it can guide you like a compass, the choice is yours. It's up to you.

When I was up there trying to figure out where I was going to die, I never once thought, I'm going to miss my Camaro, or I wish I had more time to buy a bigger house! That is just stuff. It has no value to your soul. The people in your life, relationships, kids, friends, dogs, and even strangers are important. I have a second chance at life and will build wealth and equity in my soul. I will accomplish this by treating people well, even if they don't deserve it. That's not my business or my problem.

I know what I will achieve and will use the example of what God has done for me. I'm not a preacher, pastor, or priest. I cannot impress people by throwing Bible quotes at them or writing a sermon and only giving it to people that have passed some purity test.

I will help people by showing them what God has done for me. If I succeed in my mission to Skydive again, I will use my life as an example of how God can do anything, and if you believe and work hard, you can overcome many obstacles that seem impossible to conquer. I don't want to become arrogant and think that I am somehow worthy of being used by God to show people how awesome he is, but I also don't want not to help people with the gifts given to me. I will stay humble; I'm not going to start thumping a bible around; I already said that I didn't understand most of it, and I don't have any formal theological education, and I would sound stupid, trying to act like someone I'm not. But when I succeed in my recovery, and I am Skydiving again, I won't have to say a word, and people will be able to look at me and see what God has done. I will be like a giant billboard for God, A billboard for God with a parachute on. Seeing is believing, and people will believe. I went from certain death (several times) to complete paralysis to Skydiving. That is powerful!

I know the Skydiving community is very diverse, and many people do not believe in God. That is why we never talk about religion or politics around the firepit, but you know the saying, there are no atheists in a foxhole! I don't have to preach to anyone; all I have to do is exist, live normally, show kindness toward other people, and treat everyone with dignity and respect. I will always try to help others, and Skydiving is just the icing on the cake. It proves the power of believing. I will not say that "I was Lucky" anymore. I wasn't lucky; I am blessed and grateful for it, and I will not feel embarrassed admitting it.

I hope what I have written is understood. I want to be as straightforward as possible; we are all special in God's eyes. I am no better than the homeless guy living under the bridge. When I say that I am blessed, I believe we are all blessed, but we must accept it; I asked to be saved twenty-five seconds before impact, and I think that I would have died had I not asked for help. My experience was incredible, and I have a video of it. Ok, back to my story.

Sorry for the detour. Buckle up my story is just beginning!

Chapter 10

We got home around 10 pm, and I could hear my dog, Whiskey howling as soon as I got out of the truck. Whiskey was an eight-year-old, one-hundred-and-ten-pound Alaskan Malamute, and this was by far the longest we had been apart. I had been gone for the last seven and a half weeks, and I should have been reuniting with two dogs, Gunner and Whiskey; this accident had taken so much from me. I know that without a doubt that, had I been home, Gunner would not have died. I believe the stress of me not being there and my family's overall stress killed her. Gunner was thirteen years old.

Whiskey is a very talkative malamute; sometimes, he howls in the middle of the night when the moon is out. It sounds like a train whistle. He sleeps in our master bathroom on the ledge around our tub; his full name is Wayah Moonshine Whiskey; Wayeh is the name of the breeder; Moonshine is the name of the litter; Whiskey is his name, and he is probably the closest thing to a wolf, other than a wolfdog.

What big teeth you have, grandma, better to eat you with, sweetie!!

Whiskey has big, sharp teeth and giant wolf claws, but he is a big baby, like an oversized furry pillow, with teeth. He is an excellent hunter and catches about three gigantic groundhogs a year. I missed that dog. I understand dogs more than I understand people.

It was good to be home, and I realized how much I missed my kids. They were a little mad at me for getting hurt, they were young, and I get it, I do. They were scared; I knew they would get over it, but now wasn't the time to handle it. I had work to do and intended to start it the following day. I took a shower, and I went to bed. That first night home, I slept like a rock; I didn't get woken up every two hours by loudspeakers, alarms, patients yelling for the nurses, nurses congregating at the nurse's station, or having to be catheterized or flipped over every two hours.

I woke up and immediately went to work, I needed to find a place to start therapy, and it would not be easy. The first place I tried was a well-known rehabilitation franchise. I walked in and immediately knew that it wouldn't work for me. Patients were walking in and going right for the treadmill or stationary bike with their water bottles in their hands; they looked way too comfortable, and there were no cries of pain or sudden shrieks of agony.

What the hell? Not for me, I needed to be pushed to my limits constantly. I thought of the Rocky movie, but I'm unsure which one. Three or four. Four, it was Rocky Four, the one where Appollo Creed gets killed while fighting the Russian Boxer Ivan Drago, and Rocky goes to the mountains in Russia to train for the fight. That was me. "I must break you," in my best Russian accent!

They say that with a spinal cord injury, you make most of your gains in the first six months, and after a year and a half to two years, you stop making significant gains. I was in a race against time, and I was nervous. It took me a few weeks, but I found a place, it was about an hour away from my house, but it was worth the trip. Since Kristin would not return to work till September, it was perfect. She could take me every day.

Kristin had been called into her Superintendent's office, and it was decided that she would take a leave of absence. They approved the use of her sick time to stay home and take care of me. Kristin had been teaching in the same district since she had graduated college twenty-three years earlier, and everyone was highly supportive of her. They were there for her when she needed them most, and what else could you ask for? That is the sign of good leadership when you don't have to ask for help; they know what is needed and offer it.

I appreciated it, I knew how much this inconvenienced everyone, and I felt terrible, but I was/is and always will be there for everyone, all the time, and it was nice to see that I had people in my corner. It's times like this when you get to see who is there for you, not that I was keeping track, I wasn't, but I was taking notice.

The physical therapy office that I found was Advanced Therapy in Riverdale, N.J., and it felt like I had never left the hospital. I had an initial evaluation with Dr. Christine, and she was terrific. I would have a physical therapist, a physical trainer, and a follow-up with a chiropractic doctor four times a week. The physical trainer would work on me, then the therapist would, and then the Doctor would work on my neck and back. I had some grueling sessions, but I improved fast; the pain in my hands was holding me back. My hands would get fatigued, then lose all feeling; they would keep me up at night, but the summer was almost here, and I couldn't wait to go to my home drop zone and see everyone.

When I wasn't at therapy, I spent most of my time sitting in a chair in my office, looking out the window. I would stare at a tree on the side of my house. I took a picture of that tree from my office window every time the season changed. I have a photo taken in spring 2021, summer 2021, fall 2021, winter 2021/22, and Spring 2022. I would sit there and reflect on my life. I got deep into the woods of my mind. I wanted so badly to be recovered, back in the air, and back in my life.

I remembered a job we did years ago. We assisted the Passaic County Prosecutors Narcotic/Gang Task Force. We had about seventy-five detectives from all over the County, hitting about twelve locations inside a housing project in Paterson.

I was in the lead van. It was the County Special Weapons team's van, Special Weapons and Tactics (SWAT); the Lieutenant that named me "Min Diesel" was geared up with his team inside and calling the shots. As we were rolling in, the team members were "in the zone," and I kept messing with one of the guys on the team that I was friends with. I tried to break his concentration and get him to laugh, but the Lt. kept telling me to knock it off; of course, I didn't listen, and he said to me that I would "pay" I knew what that meant, but at the time, I was having too much fun to care.

We turned the corner and started to head in with about fifteen vehicles behind us; as soon as we cleared the entranceway, people started running. I opened the door and started running myself. It was like the running of the bulls in Spain. However, we were in the SWAT van, which was higher than the standard vans, so when I jumped out and started running, my feet weren't on the ground yet, and I busted my ass and hit the pavement hard. At the same time, the van's side door opened, and the SWAT team came running out; each one used me as a step stool. As the last Officer stepped off me, I tucked and rolled, stood up, and started chasing someone as if I didn't miss a beat.

I thought to myself, Man, I hope nobody else saw that. I will never live that down.

We went from target to target until around midday and regrouped at a local fire department. I was standing there eating a sandwich and thinking to myself, I think I'm in the clear. Nobody has said a word. So, as I was standing there, a detective that I had never seen before walked up and said, hey, how's it going?

Good. What's up?

Where you in the lead van?

Oh shit, here we go.

Yeah, why, what's—I never got to finish my sentence.

He turns around and yells to a group of people, "It was him!"

As he was laughing his ass off, he explained that they were in a surveillance apartment, and not only had they seen the whole thing, but they had also filmed it; he thanked me, hugged me, and shook my hand, still laughing as he walked away.

I knew that I was in for a long night ahead of me!

Later that night, when everything was wrapped up, we all met at Paul's bar in Clifton, N.J., and of course, the story of me being used as a step stool was being told but let me hold up and give a little back, story.

We call my buddy Lenny, Big Lenny because, well, he's "Big."

But back then, he was really big, like competition big. His chest was so big that when he laughed hard, his chest would cut off the air supply at his neck, or vice versa, and he would pass out. We called it the "Huckabee."

The story was being told by Jose, whom I had nicknamed the Cuban Fatback or the Cuban Hillbilly(that's a story in itself). Big Lenny starts laughing so hard he starts doing the "Huckabee," passes out, and goes down, but on his way down, he hits the cigarette machine and knocks it over. Lenny's on the ground turning blue, and everyone is too busy stealing the packs of cigarettes the machine is spitting out to help him.

Paul's bar was a typical safe "Cop" bar. The bar had a few bowling lanes in the back room, it was so much fun, and you didn't have to wear the dreaded bowling shoes.

I sit in my chair, thinking back on my life, wondering if I can ever live a normal life again. I have been to the drop zone, and everyone has been terrific with me, but I just don't fit in. I don't know why. I know that I am still in bad shape. I limp, I'm. hunched over, but these people are my friends, aren't they? Yes, I think they are, but I was never one to believe all that "Sky family" nonsense. Yes, we were friends, but everyone was half my age, and people were busy. They have stuff going on in their own lives.

One of the hardest things to come to terms with is when you realize that some people that you care about and think of as good friends don't really care about you at all; I learned that the hard way sitting in the hospital. I just thought a few more Skydivers would at least have sent me a text.

As I said, I was much wiser when I left the hospital.

I have friends that I have been through the fire with, I still have my high school friends, and I still have my cop friends; these people are family, I can call them at three in the morning, and they would be there for me. I have been called many times at two in the morning when one of my high school buddies was in a Police station somewhere for doing stupid stuff and acting like an idiot; I showed up, always. Please don't misunderstand. I have Skydiver "friends," but when I consider someone a friend, I give it all and don't ask much in return. I'm not a fool or a doormat either, and when it becomes too one-sided, I move on with no drama.

"Good friends are hard to find but easy to lose!"
—Gary Pacelli

The summer came, and I worked my butt off. I tried to speed my recovery up, but my hands were still bad; if I held something and looked away, it would still fall out of my hands. My hands felt gigantic, and they looked weird. They felt like I was wearing those giant, "I'm number 1," hands, and they looked like claws; my fingers went off in different directions, so I hid them whenever possible. I was stiff, and my neck and back muscles and right shoulder were still locked up. It had been four months since my accident.

I currently hold a level C Skydiving license. A, C- license allows me to go six months without jumping before my license goes un-current; going un-current is usually not a big deal, although I have never not been "current."

However, if I allowed myself to go uncurrent, it would have been almost impossible to get an instructor to take me on a recurrency jump or even have a drop zone allow me to jump. I had already been told I needed a doctor's note before jumping. That will be no small task, and I still had not seen my gear.

I was starting to feel like a teenager that stayed out too late and had his car keys taken away. I didn't understand the reason for not having my gear.

It's like when I was a Detective involved in the shooting; I had to turn my weapon over to my Chief. The Sheriff sent me to the Range the following week to have a new weapon issued to me. They found that taking away an Officer's weapon after a shooting makes them feel like they did something wrong and increases the risk of Officers committing suicide after shootings. When I got to the Range, the Range Master refused to issue me a weapon. He claimed that I was out injured, and he was not permitted to qualify someone that was out injured; therefore, he would not issue me a weapon. The Sheriff called him and told him that if I wasn't given a weapon immediately, he would remove him from the Range, take his weapon and issue it to me. I was issued a weapon instantly, and he qualified me also.

I felt the same way about not having my gear. I felt as if I had done something wrong and that I was being punished. I already made it clear that I wanted to return to skydiving safely, the right way; however, if no one would help me return the right way, I was not opposed to returning the "wrong way" I could have very easily snuck off to a faraway drop zone, rented gear and jumped or acquired a base jumping rig and found a spot and hoped for the best and let it fly! I was going to jump one way or the other.

"The hardest thing in skydiving is the ground."
—Min Diesel

I understand my accident was horrific, and even though I was miles from where I was when I got rolled off that chopper, I was still in bad shape. Still, since I had made so much progress, I had fooled myself into believing I was close to being "normal"; I was on a collision course with disaster.

I was frustrated; I went to bed every night, wondering if I had reached maximum progress. I could be stuck in the condition I was in for the rest of my life. I realized why I didn't fit in; I was a spectator. I was not a participant. My world, my life, was passing me by at full speed. Everyone around me was moving forward, and I was stuck. I had a long way to go, and I saw the veterans jumping; some were missing limbs; when should I start living my life? A year? Two years? Ten? When?

Now!

I called up Shauna; Shauna is a real friend, not a drop zone acquaintance, and we have a lot in common. She is a Marine, a State Trooper, my rigger, a pilot, and the United States Parachute Association Regional Safety Director. I'm sure I left things out, many things. Shauna is the DZM, Drop Zone Manager at Skydive Shenandoah. I trust Shauna with my gear.

I trust Shauna's opinion. You may not like what she is telling you, but inside you know that she is right. I trust Shauna with my life.

I called her up. I was stressing about my gear, losing currency, and thinking no one would help me get back into the sky; I was going through a lot, both physically and mentally. Everyone avoided me; they feared I would ask for help getting back in the air. Some important people had already decided I would never jump again, and no one talked to me. Everyone spoke to me, but no one talked to me. No one knew where I was in my recovery, and no one would discuss moving forward. As I mentioned, some veterans jumped that were missing limbs; they had to modify their gear and train how to do things differently. I couldn't get anyone to work with me or discuss the possibility.

In everyone's defense, it was mid-July, probably the busiest it was going to get, and no one had time. This is not a poor me, blame game rant. There is blame and shame, and it all falls on my shoulders. My jumping situation was on me, I put myself in this position, and it was no one else's responsibility. I may have to find a drop zone that wasn't as busy, yes, that sucked, but if you want it bad enough, you will do what needs to be done.

So, I called Shauna asking about my gear, and she was great. She understood. She needed more time to fix my gear, but she said she would get it done; I needed a doctor's note, and if I got one, she would take me on a recurrency jump down at Skydive Shenandoah in Virginia at the end of August. Perfect.

I immediately called Dr. Bagin, spoke to his physician's assistant, and explained my situation. I received an email an hour later with a note from the Doctor stating, "It is my medical opinion that Gary Pacelli may engage in any and all physical activity." I was good to go!

I still couldn't figure out how to use a fork, I still needed help getting dressed, I could not tie my shoes, I had to use elastic shoelaces and slip my sneakers on and off, and I could not button my pants or shirts. I was very stiff and hunched over. I was worried that the longer it took to get back in the air, I would have more time to remember my accident, and fear would eventually creep in. People say that fear is good for you; it keeps you alert and prepared, but I don't see it this way. Fear can paralyze you and stop you from making quick decisions and acting upon them.

Caution is good. Caution will keep you prepared and alert. Once fear creeps in, it is hard to flush it out. I needed to get "back on the horse." If I lost currency, I might never get it back; this whole situation was getting to me, affecting my personality, and Kristin saw what I was going through. I didn't know it then, but she had reached out to Shauna and thanked her for all her help. She told her how important it was to me to get back up I n the air and that we appreciated it. I was falling back into a dark, nasty depression, and I needed help.

Kristin asked me to seek professional help, my nightmares were getting worse, and she would have to wake me up a few times a night. I would be drenched in sweat, yelling and screaming in my sleep; it was always the same. Most of the time, I could remember my dreams, which were usually terrifying. For example, I would suddenly be trapped in the MRI tube or back in the hospital, completely paralyzed. The nasty ones were me floating around at altitude and feeling that heavy dread of being about to die. These dreams probably don't sound scary, but the frightening thing about them was that they weren't dreams; they were memories!

Then throw in the standard issue cop nightmares that every Police Officer who has done any work experiences. My standard issue nightmare always has me fighting, nasty stuff, violent, and raw. Fighting for my life, guys coming at me with knives, baseball bats, gunfights, and avoiding being run over by cars. My favorite one is when things are bad, and you pull your weapon, people are shooting at you, and you aim and fire; at this point, it's either that I can't pull the trigger, or I pull it, and the bullet rolls out of the barrel.

I didn't want to talk to a therapist, not because I was against it; it was just that I didn't think they would understand. They couldn't truly understand my Skydiving situation, and then throw in my shooting, I didn't know if they would get it, and I was worried that they would judge me, and there was no way that I was going on head meds.

I compromised; I reached out to Brian Germain. Brian is one of the pioneers in the sport of Skydiving. He is a world-champion skydiver, test pilot, and trained in psychology. Brian has been skydiving for at least thirty-six years and has over fifteen thousand jumps. I had previously done some canopy coaching with Brian, and I had read his books, the one that was relevant to me at this time was, "Transcending Fear, the Doorway to Freedom," he also wrote another great book, "The Parachute and its Pilot."

I knew Brian would "get it," and I wouldn't have to waste all my time explaining Skydiving or adrenaline to someone.

Brian was cool; he helped me more than you can imagine by discussing my accident. I had never really discussed my accident with anyone. I told my story and what happened about 1,000 times, but I never talked about it. It's just that it's a dark, deep subject. It helped me tremendously to talk about the details, like, what I was thinking right before I hit the ground or what was going on in my mind when I was floating around. I wouldn't discuss this with Kristin; it was too painful to bring her back to that time, and I couldn't do that to her.

Most people can't or won't understand when you go through an accident like I just went through, and you are dealing with multiple handicaps. Everyone treats you as if you are invisible, and they think you have suddenly lost your ability to think. It gets to you. You want to scream; I noticed that people would generally avoid me, which was usually done subconsciously except for a few people who did it openly. I realized that it wasn't personal (for almost everyone) but think about it: you are about to board a plane that you plan on jumping out of two and a half miles off the ground. And right before you get on the plane, you see Gary, all mangled up, limping, and hunched over. You've heard about my accident, and you have either spoken to me and know the truth, or you have heard about it from some chirper that doesn't know what happened. Hey, but never let the truth get in the way of a good story!

All the planning and preparation you did for that jump goes right out the window if you let my accident get in your head. I can understand looking back on it now, but I didn't realize it then.

I remember the 1980 Winter Olympics in Lake Placid, New York. I remember the famous ski jump and how the Skiers would see a cemetery on their way down the jump; it's how people must have felt about seeing me. I was their cemetery.

Now one thing about skydivers and athletes in general, everyone can do everything better than you. And it's very rare to have someone tell you about what you did right unless you're a young, attractive female skydiver.

Everybody always tells me how I messed up my canopy deployment. I didn't slow down enough; I was head down, all correct, but very few people would say how impressive it was that I could make it back to the Drop Zone with a broken neck, paralyzed, using my head. I'm not patting myself on my back, screw it, somebody has to, Ha! but it took extreme intestinal fortitude to stay calm, focused, and determined to make it back to the DZ, and how hardcore it was that I didn't say a word the entire time.

Even when I had my shooting incident with the DEA, I could have sat on the side of the highway afterward and waited for the ambulance. I didn't; I got in my car and tried to get in the pursuit. Few people mention that it was impressive not to say a word when I was facing certain death, dancing with the Reaper, except for the military people; the Vets always would bring that up. They understand. They understand, discipline, and courage; they know Honor, and they get it and appreciate raw toughness. I was told by a few people, primarily veterans, that I had Balls of steel! It's not how hard you hit that makes you tough; it's how hard you can get hit and get up and keep fighting. Always get up and fight, get up and fight till your last breath, till the lights go out.

Never give up!
Never give in!
Never leave anyone behind!

So, I was going to be jumping in four weeks, I couldn't believe it, and I didn't believe it. I figured someone would intervene and stop it, so I kept up with my therapy, and I didn't tell anyone but Kristin, of course. I laid low and tried to keep the fear from creeping in. I had to get an open-face helmet. There was no way that I was ready to put my full-face helmet on; even thinking about it would start to freak me out. I still had bouts of claustrophobia, especially if my hands were in a lot of pain. When my hands were in pain, I would lose most of my strength in my fingers. If I was driving and the windows were open, I was fine, but if they were closed, I would have to pull over and get out, or if I were in bed, I would have to get up and open the door to my bedroom, and if they were terrible, I would have to get in a hot shower and let the water hit the back of my neck. That would always calm my nerves down and lessen the pain in my hands. I had been told that after my shooting, I probably caught a nasty case of PTSD, I disagreed, but I'm not so sure anymore.

Chapter 11

I have had many occasions when I was afraid and had to put it out of my head and do my job; back in my time, we would call that courage.

I remember the first day I reported for duty, assigned to County Patrol on the 4 pm to 12 p.m. shift. I was ready. I had my Batman utility belt shined up with all the latest approved equipment. I didn't think it was a lot. I had my weapon, two extra ammo magazines, a handcuff case, a flashlight, and a collapsible baton. All the old-timers were making fun of me. All they had was their weapon, ammo, and handcuffs, not in a case, just dangling off their belt. They said all I need is my two fists and my weapon. You shouldn't be out here if you need anything more than that.

Ok, pipe down, tiger; somebody's taking too much testosterone! I thought, what a bunch of idiots. Being prepared is not the same as being afraid. It's the exact opposite because I know that I am prepared, and I am confident that I can handle what comes my way.

One day while I was sitting in my chair, staring out the window, waiting for my big day, I remembered things from my job. I was trying to stay positive and remind myself about all the training that I had had and how I had kept my cool throughout my career. I remembered the first Sheriff I worked for and how he was elected every three years for something like nine terms. He did it by giving his voters what they wanted, safety.

As you walked into the Passaic County Jail, there was a sign. It was huge; it read, "Don't be a pimple on the ass of progress," and next to that read, "Welcome to the Passaic County Jail, this is not a Country Club!" It certainly was not a Country Club. The newspaper tried to do a hit piece on the Sheriff once for the overcrowded conditions in the jail, and they asked him to respond to the allegations. The Sheriff replied, and I quote, "I will stack them like cordwood if I have to," The Jail was built for seven-hundred inmates, and during the summer months, they would house up to two-thousand-five hundred, with no air conditioning, and they never had a problem. Leadership, training, hard work, and giant German Shepherds kept everything running smoothly.

When Jose and I were partners on the Motorcycle Squad, we were squared away; we were highly trained riders and used Gold Wing motorcycles. And even though they were not certified police bikes, we could do almost anything you could do with a Harley Davidson. We would always take some friendly abuse from the Paterson Police motorcycle squad. We would work with them constantly. Our Gold wings were painted black with the gold Sheriff's star. The Sheriff would tell us that if we rolled up on a corner and the drug dealers and gang bangers didn't automatically run, then we weren't doing our jobs, and he would replace us, and he meant it. We had ten full time riders and ten part-time riders on our squad and had to ride mirror to mirror all the time. That's why the Gold Wings were great. You could be cruising up the highway at 100 mph, riding mirror to mirror, and having a normal conversation. They were so smooth and quiet. They blew heat in the winter, and you could ride eight to ten hours daily without a problem. We rode every day if it wasn't raining and the temperature was thirty-three degrees and above. We had great hours, 10 am to 6 pm, Weekends and Holiday's off.

We were sharp, we all had to wear the same sunglasses and gloves, and we had to keep our pens in our right boots. We wore knee-high $400 motorcycle boots, Black riding britches with a gold stripe down the leg, Fall, Winter, and Spring. We wore a three-quarter length leather jacket with a black mock neck long sleeve shirt with PCSD embroidered on the collar. If I pulled you over wearing that uniform, you would swear I was about 6'4." I felt invincible. We had it good, and we worked our asses off.

I wondered if I was up for this jump, there was so much more than just jumping involved. I would have to drive five hours and get a hotel. Was I ready to be alone with no one there to help me? I knew I was overthinking it or was I? I had started seeing a neurologist, and she seemed like she got it; she was a marathon runner, so she understood drive and determination. She explained that it was a miracle that I had come this far and that there was just no information on what to expect in my stage of recovery. She said that their idea of full recovery is transferring me from the walker to the chair in the shower; that is a full recovery.

I wouldn't accept that. Other people must have broken their necks like I did and recovered more than I did. She said there most likely is, but it is so rare that there is no documentation. I searched the internet; I couldn't find any documentation, but I found YouTube videos. I found this video about an Olympic Freestyle Skiing coach; He had a similar injury and caught it on his GoPro, just like I did. I watched his recovery; it brought chills up my spine; it was so similar.

She also told me of a person in the Bahamas lying on a paddleboard in shallow water. A wave runner came screaming by, made a wake, and knocked him off the board. He broke his neck, and it took the helicopter too long to get to Miami. He is a quadriplegic now, paralyzed from the neck down.

Or,

Another person that was working on his car when he slipped off one of those creepers with the wheels on it, and he's paralyzed from the neck down,

Or,

Another person that slipped in the show— Ok, I get it enough, I'm not them, I'm me, and I'm here, and I will improve.

As the big day drew near, I stopped therapy a week before; I didn't want to be sore, and my mind began remembering random events. It seemed as if it was searching for something.

I remembered graduating from the Police Academy on a Friday Night and receiving my orders in the Lobby of the auditorium of the Passaic County Technical School. There were recruits from most of the sixteen towns in Passaic County that had just graduated. Ten of us from the Sheriff's Department; we received our orders from the Undersheriff, three of us went to the County Patrol Division, and the rest went back to the courthouse. Jose, his twin brother Lazaro and I were to report to work the next night and be assigned to the Paterson Police Task Force. There had been an accidental police shooting, and the suspect had died. The city was erupting in violence, and the Sheriff was going to assist the Paterson Police Department with whatever they needed.

At least they waited till we graduated to put us to work. I am a certified commercial diver. I got certified at a school in Long Beach, California, called the College of Oceaneering. I was 19 at the time. I was on the Sheriff's Emergency Response Team (SERT), Dive team. Two weeks earlier, I was activated and called in to recover a drowning victim that fell through the ice on the Passaic River. At the time, I was one of two divers that had ever done an ice dive, and this was an ice dive at night, so I got called in. I spent the night looking for a body under the ice, fighting a strong current, getting tangled up in shopping carts, and bumping into stolen cars while freezing my butt off in complete darkness.

The river was always black, and I welcomed it. The last thing I wanted to see was the face of a dead teenage drowning victim; there are things that you cannot unsee no matter how much Jack Daniels you drink. At least this was winter, and the water was cold; cold water dramatically slowed down the decomposition process. Usually, we would get called out in the summer, and most of the time, they were floaters. Floaters were the worst, the body would decompose, and gas bubbles would form, bloating the body and making it float to the surface. The eyes, nose, lips, ears, and fingertips would be gone; the fish eat them first.

So, you find your body. It was always pitch dark, but I kept my eyes closed anyway; I would do everything by touch. You then bring the body to the surface, and usually, once you get to the surface, all the person's skin falls off. It pops off, and you find yourself submersed in a skin smoothie. Disgusting, we were in dry suits and full-face regulators, but you never shake the thought of getting it on you. The person is locked in whatever position they were in when rigor mortis set in, so getting them into the boat was extremely difficult. To top it all off, the Passaic River at the time was highly polluted and toxic; I hated being on that team, but there was no way off it.

The Academy Director and the Assistant Director were super pissed at me for being called into work; what was I supposed to do? It wasn't up to me. I wasn't going to tell my Captain that I wasn't coming; I gave them his phone number and told them to keep me out of it, this was between them, and I hadn't slept at all, so I wasn't in any shape for the nonsense.

We reported for duty the night after graduation and got issued whatever gear we didn't have. At the time, we were not authorized to carry OC (pepper spray) individually, but they were issuing family-size OC containers to Corporals and above; they were the size of fire extinguishers. They were used for crowd control in case of a riot in the jail. Since all three of us had been with the department for over three years and were all on the SERT team, we had all our gear ready to go.

We were teaming up with the Paterson PD, and there would be three teams, each team consisted of ten cars with three officers in each, and we would be under the command of the Task Force Commander. There was a curfew in effect, so anyone on the street was to be "arrested." I use that word lightly; understand that every person we arrested would take at least one officer out of service, and within two hours, the Task Force would be off the streets; things went down a little differently. First off, everybody ran whenever they saw us, and we would catch them, then we would politely convince those fine young gentlemen that it would be in their best interest to go home and stay home, and that's how it went down, all night, for two nights in a row. I swear that's how it happened, really! Sort of.

Ok, it was a giant shit show; they ran, we chased them, we caught them, they received a major ass whooping, and we moved on to the next corner; as the night dragged on and we got a little tired, we would pull up to the corner, roll the windows down and with the family-sized OC can, we just blasted the entire corner and kept moving, it was a drive-by. No arrests, no reports, just good old superior force, and it worked. On the third night, there was a large protest outside City Hall, and it was about to get out of hand; the higher-ups had had enough, and they called in the Goon squad from the parking garage behind the building. Outcomes around a hundred highly trained, highly motivated, and extremely disciplined Sheriff's Emergency Response Team Riot Squad Officers. They set themselves up in front of City Hall. The protest was dispersed; this was 1995, and things were different. There were no cell phones. You didn't mess around. There was a code between the police and the criminal element; if both sides operated within their lanes, things never got too out of control. A year earlier, I had been called in for another riot; this one was a little different,

The Italians on 21st Ave were going nuts, it was July 17th, 1994, and the World cup was being hosted in Pasadena, California. It was Italy vs. Brazil, the game ended in a tie and the winner was decided in a penalty shootout. Italy lost 3-2, and the Italians on 21st Ave were out in the streets, flipping garbage cans and making a lot of noise; they were pissed.

21st Avenue, in Paterson then, was considered the Italian section. I was born in Paterson, NJ. My family lived on 48 Webster Ave, surrounded by all my aunts, uncles, cousins, and close family friends. I lived there till I was five, and my family moved out into the "country" to a small town about forty minutes north. My grandparents still lived on the first floor of that house. My entire family was from Paterson.

We staged at the firehouse on 21st Avenue, and the Sheriff decided that since they weren't doing any significant damage and were only damaging their own homes and businesses, they would be allowed to blow off some steam and let the homemade wine wear off. That's precisely what happened; they stayed up all night cleaning up the mess they had made and spent the next three months apologizing and trying not to let us pay for our meals in their restaurants. What a time to be a cop!

I'm not comparing the two incidents', apples and oranges, one was over the accidental death of a young man, and the other was a case of too much wine and the loss of a game. You cannot compare the two. I was just involved in both. No judgments.

Chapter 12

I mentioned earlier that we were not allowed to carry OC pepper spray individually. That changed sometime around 1997. We all got trained and certified. To be certified, you had to get sprayed in the face and be able to function, use your baton, talk on the radio, and draw your weapon. Getting sprayed is not fun. You can't see, it's hard to breathe, and your skin is on fire. I was lucky and knew what to expect from going through the "gas chamber" on Parris Island during boot Camp. Even still, you never really get used to it. The SERT Commander, Captain Dykstra (real name), oversaw certifying everyone and keeping track of who was using it. We had a special report to fill out every time it was used.

We were having a typical morning. I was a Corporal and second in command of the Motorcycle Squad by now; Jose had been promoted to Detective and gone to narcotics, and I had a new partner, JP. JP was the best; everybody loved JP. I have never seen him in a bad mood. More on JP later. JP was away at a school, and a few guys rode solo that day. I heard one of the guys pull a car over a few blocks away, and it came back unregistered.

On the bikes, we followed specific protocols, and we only called for backup if things got bad, fast, but we would always stay in the area of each other, especially the guys that were riding solo. We also had a particular way of calling things in on the radio, and if there were any deviations, the other squad members would pick up on it and head over; it was our way of letting the rest of the squad know that something wasn't right and that we might need a little help. So, Ray called in the plate and gave his location, but he also stated that the driver was alone. That was a sign for anyone in the area to swing by. I headed over, rolled up, and the driver was out of the vehicle talking to Ray. No problem: everything looked normal. I got off my bike and stood by. Ray was writing a few tickets. This was going to be a six-pack and a tow. A six-pack was, six tickets, and a tow was a vehicle impound. The driver was about a hundred and twenty pounds and was scratching all over. An addict. He started to get antsy, I inched my way closer from behind him, and I saw him look right, then left, and I knew.

I knew he was getting ready to run. At that moment, the dispatcher stated that the driver was 10-50; 10-50 was our radio code for wanted, they knew our codes on the street, and at that moment, I lunged for the driver. I went for the waistband on his pants, if you go for the shirt, you will be standing there with a shirt in your hand, watching your guy haul ass down the street, he bolted as soon as I went for him, but I had his waistband he wasn't going anywhere, and I had almost 100 lbs. on this guy, so I thought. This dude must have been a superhuman science project. He started dragging me down the street. Ray jumped on us. Ray was a professional bodybuilder. He was gigantic, and we went down. This guy is fighting like crazy; we are both on him. He gets up and throws us off him like we are rag dolls. This same scenario keeps playing out. We fight him, punch, kick and tackle him. He shakes us off, gets up, and drags us further down the street.

That's it. I've had enough. I yell to Ray, "Duck!" Ray yells, "Noooo!" Ray should've ducked. I sprayed both of them.

At this moment, a patrol Officer, Officer Carmello Criscione (Mel), we all used to work together in the jail, was driving down the street and saw us in the middle of the road being thrown around by this little dude. He couldn't believe what he was watching. Then he sees the dude and Ray drop. I cuffed the driver. He was crying like a baby, screaming, snot flying. It was something to see. I thought about cuffing Ray; so he didn't kill me for spraying him, but I decided against it.

Ray was mad, but he knew I had no choice. If I didn't spray him, I would have had to use my baton, which was a guaranteed hospital trip and another assault charge on my record. No way, this was the way to go. We threw the driver into the back of Mel's car and headed back to headquarters. When we arrived at HQ, the fight was out of him; he was a nice guy. He just didn't want to go to jail. We cut him some slack, processed him on his warrants, and didn't charge him with assault and resisting, which was a huge break. The day went on as usual, and I forgot about it by lunch.

Two weeks passed, and I had just finished physical training with the Police recruits. I was a Police Academy Drill instructor and Physical Fitness training instructor. I would get to the academy at five in the morning, and train the recruits, then take a shower at the academy, put my uniform on and go to work on the bikes at 10 am, it was a long day, but they took care of me with comp time.

This morning was no different from any other. I was in the instructor's locker room taking a shower, and the SERT Commander, Captain Dykstra, walked in with a bag in his hand. I said good morning, and he replied, "so, you like spraying people with your little OC can? So do I, but I like using my big can!" Captain Dykstra pulls out the family-size can from the bag and blasts me. I started choking; between the steam from the shower and the OC spray, I couldn't breathe, and my eyes were burning so much that I couldn't open them. My nose was pouring out snot, and since my pores were already opened from the hot shower, my skin was on fire. I hit the ground, and he continued to blast me as I lay on the shower floor, naked, with the hot water hitting me, keeping my pores open, allowing the OC to get in there and burn.

Captain Dykstra said, "I issued over four- hundred cans of OC. You had to be the first person to use it. Now you know what it feels like, and you better not be late for work." As he walked out of the locker room, he turned around and said, "oh, by the way, Good job, keep up the good work" he left me there, dying on the shower floor. I stayed there for what felt like an eternity.

Next time, I would be more careful and make sure my partner didn't get sprayed.

I loved that guy, and I would do anything for him. He was a mentor from the time I walked into that jail, he knew it was all foreign to me, and he looked out for me. I wouldn't be where I was without old-timers like that. They wouldn't write you up if you made a mistake. They would put you through hell till you saw the error of your ways. They were true role models and great leaders.

Captain Dykstra retired, moved to Florida, and died of cancer.

Where was I?

Oh yeah.

Show time.

Game day weekend, I got to Skydive Shenandoah Friday afternoon. I checked into my hotel and settled in for what I thought would be a sleepless night; it wasn't. I slept like a baby. I woke up, made some coffee, and got ready, waiting for something, I was prepared for anything, and I got nothing.

Skydive Shenandoah is in New Market, Virginia. It is a lovely, historic southern town nestled in the valley of Shenandoah County.

Skydive Shenandoah has since become one of my favorite drop zones; it was owned by the same owner as Skydive Sussex, Rich "Winnie" Winstock, another Skydiving Legend. Most of the people I name in this story, I could write a whole book on each of them, and their stories are incredible and should be told, who knows, maybe I will someday.

I introduced myself to everyone and found Shauna; she explained that she hadn't finished my gear yet, and I thought, here we go. Then she said that she had a student rig ready for me and that my canopy had been inspected and put into the rig. Awesome! We spoke about my upcoming jump, and Shauna wanted to ensure I understood what was at stake. She explained that after I exited and got stable, we would link up, and I would do a few turns and get comfortable, make sure that I was "altitude aware," and then wave off and deploy my canopy. Shauna explained that she would stay close if something happened, and I had trouble deploying. Great!

Shauna then explained that If I did anything unsafe or thought I wasn't ready yet, she would ground me for six months, and then we would try again.

Fair enough, I respected her thought process, and I knew that she would be sincere and give me a fair shot, there was no agenda, and I trusted her.

We would jump out of the "Shark," the legendary Shark. The Shark was a Cessna 182, a little smaller than I was used to; I wasn't sure if I was limber enough to crawl in, crouch down, and exit safely. I spoke to Shauna, and she could tell I was a little concerned; she told me not to worry, and when it came time to exit, she wanted me to swing my legs out the door and fall out. I could do that, I hoped. I hoped I didn't get inside and get claustrophobic and flip out.

I had no fear. I was nervous about how my body would be, how I would have to compensate for flying the wind and staying stable. I was worried about my body position and controlling my legs; if you lose control of a limb, it could very quickly throw you into a violent spin. Therefore, I was jumping to figure all these things out. It was showtime, and I was excited. I climbed into the "Shark," and I had a funny thought. I was jumping before I could even tie my shoes. It was five months and twelve days since my accident, and I was getting into the Shark. I was doing this, and if Shauna didn't have such confidence in me, I don't know if I would have been able to do it.

I know one thing, no one else would have taken me up. I didn't know how much she was sticking her neck out for me; I would find out later that she was taking a huge chance on me, and I don't know if I will ever truly be able to repay her! We climbed in and put our seat belts on, so far so good; it wasn't claustrophobic inside. We took the ride to altitude, and I was trying to get a bearing on where I was. We were in a valley, and the mountain views were just fantastic; Shauna pointed out the airport and gave me the thumbs up. We would be getting out shortly.

I still had no fear. I was concentrating on everything that was about to happen. Shauna opened the door, and I swung my legs out; I was sitting there with my legs dangling out of the plane over two miles high, smiling from ear to ear. I was back in action; whatever happened next would be by my hand. I was ready for this.

I'm so blessed that I can walk, and I'm so grateful that I have been given a second chance to skydive again. Shauna gives me the thumbs up. I lean forward and push myself out of the plane, the wind hits me and puts me into a flip, and I quickly recover and get stable and try to let the wind put me into a basic belly skydive position. I'm super stiff, and I start to do what is called potato chipping. I recover and relax. I let my body adjust to the wind. I turn right, then left. I don't see Shauna.

Shauna is above me, watching me, I finally see her, and she comes to me; we dock with each other and are smiling. I cannot believe I am doing this; my mind goes back to being rolled into that hospital, everyone frantically working on me, saving my life. I cannot stress how big of a deal this is to me; everything flashes in my mind like pictures flashing. It is overwhelming. The altimeter in my helmet begins to beep at 6,500 ft. I give Shauna a thumbs up. She repositions herself to my side; she's like a flying ninja. My altimeter beeps at 5,500 ft. I wave off and reach behind and deploy my canopy.

Here we go. Is the opening going to break my neck? Has my neck healed enough? Will I become paralyzed again and float around? Nope, it opens. Here it is. My lines are twisted. Twisted lines, most likely from being so stiff and having a poor body position, no big deal. I reach up and grab my risers. I can only reach up a little. My shoulders are locked, so I start scissor kicking to counteract the spin on my canopy, and thirty seconds later, my line twists are gone. I reach up and grab my toggles and do a canopy check. My canopy looks good. I turn right; I turn left; I do three practice flares, good. I'm good. I sit back in my harness and take in the view; I have time to think about my life and all the people I have been fortunate to meet and become friends with. I am truly blessed. I was floating up there, thinking about what's important and admiring the unbelievable view of the Shenandoah Valley.

I begin to laugh; I'm alive; I yell at the top of my lungs, "I'm Alive!"

Chapter 13

JP and I were planning on getting hired by the Wanaque Police Department. We secretly took the test and ranked one and two on the list. JP was a Gulf War Veteran, so he ranked number one, and I ranked number two. This all had to be done in secret. The Sheriff's Department had gotten strange; if they caught wind that we were thinking about working elsewhere, they would destroy us and sabotage our new job prospects. It was like a cult.

We got called into the Wanaque Police Department, and the Chief wanted to speak to us. Chief Reno was a no-nonsense Chief. He coached me in football when I was in grammar school, and he drove me home in 8th grade when he caught me shooting bottle rockets at houses. Chief Reno took a liking to me and JP. As we were sitting in his office, he explained that he could only hire one of us now and then hire the other one six months later. Since JP was ranked number one, it would be JP.

JP told the Chief that he would have to decline his offer of employment. I went nuts. What the hell is wrong with you? I yelled, and the Chief echoed my question. JP explained to the Chief that if he accepted the job, the Sheriff would throw me back into the jail, set me up, and that I wouldn't make it six months; they would find a way to fire me. I told JP not to worry about me, I could handle myself, and to take the damn job, but he refused.

Chief Reno got mad as hell, walked out, walked back in, lit a cigarette, and said," I don't know how I'm going to do it, but

I'll find a way. Give your two weeks' notice and get out of my office."

I think it must be a Cop thing, but we love getting in the last word and throwing ourselves out of our offices!

We left the Chief's office, and I thanked JP; what a good friend; how many people do you know that would do something like that for you? How many people do you know you would do something like that for? This is what life is about, helping each other. JP could have taken the job, and I would not have thought less of him. JP is a man of principle and honor, a major ball breaker, and a giant pain in the ass, but a man of principle and honor, nonetheless.

The next day I met JP at Headquarters. I was off that day, burning as much of my comp time as possible; I had many days saved up from working at the academy, JP was working, and we headed over to the Sheriff's Office to resign and give our two weeks' notice. We walked into the Sheriff's office, and he looked happy to see us, it was a shame that we were leaving, but the upper management had begun to lose their minds and was acting tyrannical. It was time to go, the winds of change were in the air, and my Spidey senses told me to go while the getting was good. We walked in, and JP handed him his resignation. His face turned bright red, and I thought, oh boy, this isn't going to go well. He looked at me and said, "What the hell are you doing here?" I explained that I would be giving my two weeks' notice also. He stood up. I thought he was going to throw a punch at one of us. He yelled, "two weeks? You're both fired, get out of my office, and turn your gear in."

We walked out of that office, laughing our asses off. We just got fired and weren't getting paid anymore, but we felt free.

We had to turn our gear in to Captain Dykstra in the SERT Office, we were laughing and joking, and Captain Dykstra called me over to his computer and told me to hit the "delete" button. I hit the button, and he said, that's it! You're deleted; it's as if you were never here. We turned our gear in and got the hell out of there.

I was following JP home in my car when I saw him swerve into the oncoming lane to get the attention of the Wanaque Chief. The Chief was driving in the oncoming traffic lane and pulled over when he saw JP.

He was nervous; the Sheriff was the County's most powerful law enforcement officer.

How did it go?

We got fired.

JP started to break his chops in typical JP fashion; he began with, "he's pissed at you!"

Really? I don't care, start Monday morning, 9 am, in my office.

Thanks, Chief.

You two are going to be trouble, I can tell!

We went home, changed, and headed to Rhodie's bar, right across the Wanaque border; they knew us well and always let us sit in the same spot. I held court many nights there in that corner of the bar. We had finished a bottle of Grey Goose by the time our wives, Kristin and Tina, showed up; JP was passed out on the pool table. It was the start of some fun times; we were now legends at the Sheriff's Department because we had the balls to finally do what many Officers wanted to do but couldn't. The floodgates were opened, and people started leaving like crazy. There was about to be a change; Jose's friend and narcotics partner, A retired Detective from the New York City Police Department, was going to run for Sheriff and win in two years.

I was made a Detective eight months later and had it made. The Chief loved us, and I was aggressive; everything was going great, but as I said earlier, change was in the air, and I would not escape it.

I landed my canopy on target but wasn't taking any chances. I slid my landing in, happy to have landed safely. I was so excited. I was smiling ear to ear, and Shauna was smiling even wider than me. We did it. I can't believe that we did it. Shauna cleared me, and I jumped again that day, this time alone; it was terrific. I went back to my hotel that night and had the best sleep of my life. I felt satisfied. I thought my journey was over. It had to be. The next day, I boarded the plane, jumped, and this time, I stood my landing up! Shauna filmed my landing, and now I felt terrific. The weight of the world felt like it was lifted off my shoulders. In skydiving, landing safely is the goal. Whether you slide it in or stand it up does not matter; landing safely is the only thing that matters.

But it looks cool and feels great when you stand it up, and after you snap your neck, can't move, can't walk, then five months later you stand one up, hell yeah, you're going to feel amazing. Before my accident, I had a ninety-five percent stand-up rate. It would take time, if possible, to stand my landings up consistently now. But I'm ok with that; to be able to jump again means the world to me. I just proved that if I put the work in, I could live a mostly normal life. If I can jump out of a plane and stand up a landing, I could do anything, so on those days that I'm in a whole lot of pain, and I don't feel like getting out of bed, and I want to quit, I can't, because I can do anything, suck it up and get to it.

I was in a nasty, dark place, and Shauna pulled me out; she took a chance and stuck her neck out for me. I would not be jumping if it wasn't for her. I spoke before of the old timers that were true leaders in Law enforcement or Kristin's Administration and how they showed true Leadership. Shauna did the same; she showed true Leadership in the sport of

Skydiving by not judging me and giving me a chance. We need more role models in this sport like her. Instead of walking around like a skygod, some "great" jumpers should be more willing to help others, especially jumpers returning from injuries. I asked three instructors if they would work with me and help me return safely. They all refused; I was willing to pay them. I tried to tell them that they really should humble themselves a little, we don't get to pick our battles, and the Wolf is always at the door. Especially when you think it can't happen because you're so good.

I was on top of the world. I almost thought that I was a badass. I almost took God and what he had done for me for granted. But I was the one that put the work in. I was the one that worked through the pain. How foolish of me. I'm ashamed to admit how quickly I forgot and was about to get smacked hard in the face. I think that is the problem with most of us. We forget the gifts that we are given. We forget the truly important things. God has saved me at least two times that I know of, and then I get arrogant and full of pride and forget. We forget God or are embarrassed to openly admit what has been done for us.

Just recently, I was in the Tandem Instructor tent at Skydive Sussex, and one of the staff asked me about my accident, and I told him about it. I began to tell him that I got really lucky, and as I said that, a Jumper that I know yelled across the tent and said you didn't get lucky. You are blessed.

That dude is a badass, and that was when I decided to write this book. At least four doctors told me I should write my story down, and countless others said the same. But the jumper in the tent yelled that I was blessed, and he had courage, and from that moment on, I decided to stop being afraid and stand up for God. My story gets a little spicey, and I did nothing alone. I say this all the time now; I can put my two feet on the ground and get out of bed. It's a great day, every moment, every breath is a gift, and I'm not wasting any of it. I'm not wasting it on pettiness or petty people; sometimes, people are so miserable that they must bring you down to their level. Don't fall for it; it's a trap, a pit. Pits are for snakes. Leave the snakes alone.

"The man of principle never forgets what he is because of what others are."

—Baltasar Gracian

"If you are a man or woman of principle, you live your life your way, according to your principles and beliefs, no matter how anyone else lives. You don't use the words or actions of others to justify putting your principles on a shelf or lowering your standards. You must remain true to yourself, no matter how other people behave or choose to live their lives."

—The Gentleman Warrior

I left that weekend on top of the world. I was back, I just had some kinks to work out, but I was back.

But I wasn't back for long. And what it would take after my following near-death incident was going to take every tool in my tool belt. I would have to rely on family and friends again.

I would even have to rely on new friends.

I would have to go to war with my most formidable enemy. Myself!

This time I would have to face fear.

Chapter 14

"Whether a King or a Street Sweeper, we all have to dance
with the Grim Reaper."

—-Unknown

I drove home from Skydive Shenandoah feeling completely satisfied. My return jumps, and the weekend was a total success. I got home and slipped right back into my routine, I went back to therapy and showed the therapist my landing video, and everyone was beyond excited.

I had new energy; I now had something to do on weekends. I did not have to be a spectator. I could now be a participant. I could believe nothing had happened and everything would return to the way it was.

The following weekend, I went to Skydive Sussex. I jumped once on Saturday and got hit with a crosswind. Not my best work but not terrible. I showed up early on Sunday, September 4th, and you could feel that Fall crispness in the air. I had unloaded my gear and was in the fun jumper tent. I was starting to get that uneasy feeling, exactly like I had almost six months earlier. I had watched the first few loads land and was waiting for the landing field to dry up some, there was a slight frost, and the sun had just thawed it out.

There is a saying in Skydiving: No Skydiver ever got hurt on the ground. More accurate statements have yet to be made.

I was feeling rushed and was a little worried about the temperature and how my hands would react when cold, I grabbed a pair of gloves, not thinking about it, but I did go through the trouble of cutting out the palm of the glove that I would be wearing on my right hand. My routine was all out of whack; I couldn't find my place, and I was fidgety. I knocked my water cup over, made a mess, and cleaned it up. The table my helmet and altimeters were on broke and tipped over. It was one thing after another! I had that gnawing thought again, and then I heard the "voice" in my mind telling me to take myself off the load; I knew to listen this time. I walked up to the manifest window with the full intent of removing myself from the plane. I got to the window, and instead of getting off the plane, I just said hello to everyone! What the hell was I thinking? I will tell you; I thought I was being a coward. There was nothing to worry about. I should have taken myself off the load, re-grouped, and re-evaluated my situation. I had all day; I had the rest of my life!

I returned to the tent and began to suit up, but the uneasy feeling did not go away.

And I had not learned a thing from my previous accident!

I boarded the plane and climbed to altitude, and I was nervous. I exited the plane at 13,344 feet, had a great exit, and was in an excellent stable body position. I had an incredible freefall; I was taking it all in, everything was fine, I was working myself up for nothing, and I was checking my Dekunu digital altimeter the entire way down. At 5,500 feet, I did my usual 360-degree turn to ensure that no one was above me and that my air space was clear.

I waved off, reached around, and tried to deploy my canopy, but nothing. I reached back, tried to deploy my pilot chute again, and could not grab it. I kept trying but could not feel it. This is not an excuse, just an explanation. I was expecting a dangling hackey to grasp, but I had been using a PVC handle, and it was not hanging; it was tight against my rig, and my hand just passed right over it. The deployment handle was there, but I didn't feel it, which was terrifying.

I tried too many times and got dirty low. I ignored my decision altitude and tried to deploy again, burning up precious altitude at around 1,500 feet. I realized that I had put myself in a box and was running out of options. I thought that I had more time, but I didn't. I went from 2,500 ft to 1,500 ft in what felt like a flash. The fact that I could not feel my carbon fiber PVC pilot chute handle meant that I would not be able to feel my reserve handle, and being that I was still very stiff, I was concerned about struggling with my reserve deployment handle, becoming unstable, and then having my AAD fire.

Because I would be unstable, I could end up with line twists at around 500 feet. I would not have time to clear the line twists and most likely would not survive the landing.

Since I was stable, my only chance of surviving this would be to brace myself and wait for my AAD to fire. I didn't say I hoped it would fire; I said wait for it to fire. I was confident it would work.

An AAD is an Automatic Activation Device; it is used to open your reserve parachute container at a preset altitude if a descent rate exceeds a preset activation speed.

It is a must-have. If a skydiver were to become unconscious or lose altitude awareness, the AAD would deploy his reserve canopy.

When I say wait for the AAD to fire, I'm not talking about a significant amount of time; I'm talking three, maybe four seconds at most, I was in a stable body position, and you can see that on my video. I braced, held my position, and the AAD fired and put a beautiful reserve canopy above my head.

This decision was highly controversial and an admitted horrible decision, but it was the best bad decision I had. I acknowledge that it was wrong, and I also realize that if I say anything else, people lose their minds. I weighed the pros and cons, made a decision, and carried it out; I held my body position and let my AAD fire.

Is this happening? I cannot believe this is going down like this, all that suffering and bullshit I put everyone through, not to mention everything I'd been through, to end up "going in" at my home, DZ. I was pissed. I couldn't believe it.

My plan worked perfectly. My AAD fired, and by the time my canopy deployed and finally opened, I was at 418 feet; since I had an almost eighty-second freefall, I knew exactly where I was and where I was going to try and land. My landing options were limited, so I cleared the power lines and steered to the left of a lovely red barn. I landed, and I was alive.

When we say fired, we mean fired; when your AAD goes off, it sounds like a gunshot.

I exited the plane at 13,344 ft and opened at 418 ft. I usually open at around 4,500 ft.

I was alive, but that was dangerously close; If my AAD had not worked like it was supposed to, I'd be dead. If I were over some of the rolling hills in Sussex, I'd be dead. I'd be dead if I forgot to turn my AAD on. If my aunt had balls, she'd be my uncle! We can play the "what if game all day long. I knew all these things; a series of mistakes put me in a position I could not escape.

I use a Cypress AAD; The Cypress AAD went into service in 1991. It has been along on 165 million skydives; No Cypress has ever failed to activate. The Cypress has, to date, saved over 5,200 lives. Including myself.

I was alive, but I was in major trouble. Everyone was mad at me; I had to eat a lot of shit, and some people have never spoken to me since. I felt like Frankenstein when the entire village chased him down with pitchforks and torches. I was finished.

I understand I misused my Cypress, and it was stupid to rely on a machine. However, no one was there but me. I was more upset that I didn't listen to my instincts and took myself off the plane; I was more upset that I was cocky enough to think that I could throw a glove on at that time. I was more upset that after two tries to deploy, I should have just gone to my reserve handle.

I'm a trained Marine, a Motorcycle cop, and a Detective. I have been carrying, maintaining, and relying on my equipment since I was 18. I will not carry a piece of equipment I cannot trust. I said trust, not depend on.

I took the advice, criticism, and abuse and was very humble; they were right. The book says so; some people did care about me. But after a while, the advice turned to abuse, and I let it get in my head; it was early September, and my grand comeback was over. I failed, but I was alive.

Going "in," is a term Skydivers use; it means getting killed on a Skydive; people talk about "going in" a little too casually around the firepit at night. They talk about death as if they know a thing or two about it. Most don't, and they should be careful and not take death so lightly. Some jumpers were running around, convinced I had tried to kill myself. Now, had any of them taken the time to speak to me and learn what I had just spent the last six months going through, they would realize how ridiculous of a statement that was. But I get it; it's more fun to talk shit.

> "Death? What do you all know about death?"
> —Sgt. Barnes. Platoon. 1986

I can talk shit too, but I don't.

I thought about packing it in and selling my gear, but that wasn't my style, either way, I was finished jumping for some time. I needed to get back in the gym, clear my head, and put some time and distance between myself and all the chirpers. Overconfidence almost killed me; this one came at me fast and furious, and there would be a heavy price to pay. How many lives do I have left? Some people at the drop zone were jokingly saying that I was invincible and could not be killed; that made me a little uncomfortable. But one thing I knew was that it was time for another change.

I bought a giant sandwich, went home, and watched my GoPro video. The video is insane. The ground keeps getting bigger and bigger. This episode gave me such an overload of adrenaline that it triggered my nervous system into overdrive. It messed up my central nervous system for weeks. I was in terrible shape, and winter was coming.

I have permanent nerve damage, it doesn't affect me much in warm weather, but below 65 degrees, my body begins to lock up and shake uncontrollably if I'm not dressed for the weather. I couldn't believe how fast everything that I worked for fell apart.

Here we go, back in my chair, looking out the window and crawling back into my head. I cannot believe how close I came to dying again; it was starting to get old. I felt horrible and like I had let Shauna down; she had stuck her neck out for me, and I went and blew it. I cannot tell you what it was like, to grab my harness and wait for my AAD to fire; It was like flipping a coin, heads I live, tails I die, and hit the ground at 140 mph, I bounce. I was not afraid; I had nothing to fear. The AAD was going to work, or it wasn't; if it worked, I would have a canopy over my head, or I would be "IN" in three seconds. I needed to carry out the plan perfectly. There was no room for error. A few people at the drop zone said, "I had Balls of steel!" At least a few people recognized raw courage; again, most were Vets.

I was told that I was too crazy to skydive. I would like to analyze that statement; I deliberately weighed ALL the facts regarding my situation. I took in all the information available to me, I was aware of my altitude, and I considered my current physical state and made a decision regarding a piece of equipment that has a 100% success rate, made a decision in a fraction of a second, stuck with the decision, was successful, and that makes me crazy? Not in my book.

So, if I lost altitude awareness and my AAD fired unexpectedly, that is ok? Or if I panicked and froze and my AAD fired, is that ok also? Is it that we must treat all skydivers like they are children, and there is no possible way that we can understand our equipment and utilize it to its fullest capacity? I know what I'm saying is controversial, but some of the things that were said to me were a little over the top and out of line, and I kept my mouth shut, but those days are over, and I'm not ashamed that I wasn't afraid, sorry, I have balls, and brains!

I heard through a friend of mine that it was said that I was "selfish" for jumping, that I wasn't ready to be jumping, and that I put the DZ at risk.

My response was that everyone forgets where they come from and are hypocrites; any jumper in my position would have tried to jump just like I did, and if they say otherwise, they are lying. If we helped each other and were empathetic, skydivers returning from injuries wouldn't feel like outcasts and have to sneak around for training. Also, my accident and AAD fire did not hurt anyone but me; I never put anyone else at risk or in the hospital. My friend Sam has a saying; he says that he may make mistakes, but he never makes the same mistake twice. I'm the same way.

Ok, I said my peace; I'm done, not wasting another minute on it. I'm sorry if I inconvenienced anyone, and the next time I break my neck, I promise that I will go away and no one will have to see me.

I went back to the gym; My nerves finally settled down. I needed to start from scratch, I began to be able to tie my shoelaces shortly after, and I finally learned how to use a fork again—the morning before I broke my neck. I weighed 189 lbs. and had thirteen percent body fat; I was in the best shape of my life. The day I was discharged from the hospital, I weighed 160 lbs. I had to wear my son's clothes; nothing I owned fit me.

> "Life is Hard, But it's Harder if you're Stupid."
> —John Wayne

Amen!

I needed to regroup my thoughts. I realized I could not take anything for granted; I was not owed a recovery; I needed to earn it. There were no guarantees. It was October, and I would try again in March; I would meet up with my friend Sam at Skydive City in Zephyrhills, Florida.

Sam Kidstar is my friend. Sam is a union Iron Worker who usually works on the skyscrapers in New York City; everywhere he goes, he has his two Quacker Parrots with him, Baby and Precious; those birds are incredible. I never knew how intelligent birds are. They are probably smarter than a few people that I know.

Sam is a wingsuit guy; he has over 2,800 jumps. He travels all over the country, working and visiting new drop zones; he has jumped at over thirty so far.

Shauna fixed my gear, and I went into deep hibernation. I couldn't understand why I was under such an attack. That is precisely how I felt, under attack. I would make progress, and then I would be laid low. I read a book on spiritual warfare, which said that whenever you submit to God, you get attacked

131

by the adversary, to have you lose faith. It sure felt like I was being attacked, but that tells me I was over the target. That's how the bomber planes in World War 2 knew they were over the target; when the enemy flack got bad, they knew to release their bombs. Everyone thinks this world is a playground; I think of this world as more of a battleground.

It's like the box that I'm supposed to be in at my age. When you get out of your box, you open yourself up for attack; stay in your box! I'm not going down that way. If God is for us, who can be against us? Right? That's having strong backup! I could just be too stubborn to quit, I don't think so; committed, yes.

I think of all the people who have criticized me and judged me, and I hoped and prayed that they never get tested as I did. I wish they would humble themselves a little; this way, they don't have as far to fall when they get their turn on the Wheel of Misfortune. This entire situation has taken its toll on me; this trip to Florida was a make-or-break moment. If I failed, it was over; I would be sentenced to the couch and endless driveway drinking.

I sold my Camaro and bought a little travel trailer; I needed the trailer to escape the cold weather in the winter, as my nerves could not handle the cold. I had spoken to Shauna; she offered me a job doing ground crew work for the upcoming season at Skydive Shenandoah; I was excited, but I hoped I could physically handle the work.

I was heading down to Florida at the end of February, staying for almost three weeks, jumping with Sam, then heading to South Carolina for a few days to see Lenny, then heading to Skydive Shenandoah for safety day and dropping off the trailer. I was looking forward to that trip; I had a great campsite sixty feet from the beach in South Carolina.

I had four months to think and reflect; I was tired. Was any of this worth it?

I just transferred back to the Sheriff's Department, and they sent me out to a few schools, HIDTA 1 and Top Gun. They were both narcotics Officer training schools; HIDTA stands for High-Intensity Drug Trafficking Area. They were both great training courses. While in Top Gun, I got a call from my Chief. A Chief ran my unit, and he answered directly to the Sheriff. There was no one in between. Chief Murray explained that a guy kept calling the TIP line and eventually got in touch with the Sheriff and had information on someone selling narcotics in Passaic, N.J. The Sheriff promised that it would be handled, and since I was the new guy and no one else wanted it, the job was mine as soon as I got back from the course I was taking.

When I returned from school, I started surveillance daily, watching who showed up at the condo and writing down the vehicle license plates. I would watch people bring bags out of the apartment and resist the urge to stop the vehicles and make an arrest for instant gratification, but I knew I had a good case here. All the players had a criminal record for narcotics, and this was an active spot.

I presented my findings to the Chief, who liked my work so far; still, he knew I was inexperienced, so he teamed me up with a Lieutenant and a Detective from the Prosecutor's Office. Lieutenant "Bobby" and Filthy Frank had personally run past cases on this target. This is how I met the Lieutenant that named me "Min Deisel." They wanted my case file; there was no way I was turning all my work over, a month of complex, hard surveillance. The Chief called a truce and ordered us to work the case together. I was good with that, and they warmed up to the idea.

We immediately went to work. I liked both of them, Bobby made his bones with the Paterson Police Department before transferring to the Prosecutors Office, and Frank had just spent the last ten years assigned to the DEA, writing wiretap affidavits and doing huge cases. I was in good hands, and I loved to argue with Frank, but that was ok; he hated everyone. The Lieutenant had gone to the Police Academy with Lenny. They started on the streets together. He was a lunatic, and I say that with the utmost respect; he was a Marine and hardcore.

We very quickly were up on a wiretap; One wire turned to three, and it was busy; the case turned into a monster. A simple narcotics case turned into a giant can of worms; we had organized crime, kidnapping, and attempted murder, and some influential people were snagged on our wire.

The core group of knuckleheads were a bunch of wannabe mobsters; they did have organized crime connections, but these guys were cop magnets, acting on their own. One night while we were supervising the wire room, a few of the idiots and one that we had nicknamed the Aardvark. We called him that because of the size of his nose, so the Aardvark and his crew steal a bread truck in Manhattan. The driver was doing his delivery route, and they yanked him out of his truck and drove around Manhattan throwing rolls at people and hitting people over the head with loaves of bread. You cannot make this stuff up; absolutely hilarious.

They were on the phone the whole time, and then they called the "Ringleader." In Passaic, N.J., We will call him, Caluso: they called him up; this was one of the funniest things I have ever heard on a wire:

Aardvark: Hey, we just had a major score!
Caluso: What do you got?
He was excited! This could be the big one.
Aardvark: We're rolling in dough.
Caluso: what did you hit? A jewelry store?
Aardvark: We got tons of bread! Were set.
Caluso: Bro, what do you have?
Aardvark: We got Focaccia, French, rolls, loaves, everything.

Caluso: What the hell are you talking about?

Aardvark: We just stole a bread truck; we were hungry

Caluso: You guys are fucked up.

Caluso hangs up the phone. We cannot stop laughing. It was like watching a movie. I started to have a slight fondness for these idiots after that; say what you want. They were funny.

They would get on the phone and say, I just saw the twins. I think they're following us; we better not talk on the phone, then they would make plans to buy "Special K"; it was amazing.

A week later, these same maniacs kidnapped the boyfriend of the ex-girlfriend of one of the guys in their crew. This dummy kept a duffle bag containing one hundred and fifty thousand dollars at his ex-girlfriend's house. Her current Junkie boyfriend found it, went to Atlantic City, and spent it all on hookers and coke.

The Caluso gang thought it was a good idea to chain him up in the gym they worked out in, keep him there for about a week, and beat him half to death with dumbbells.

When we took this wire down and arrested the crew that wasn't already locked up, we grabbed them in the Bergen County Mall. The main target, Caluso, was in a restaurant with his girlfriend, and when he saw us coming, he bolted. This dude was in shape, and we chased him throughout the mall. Finally, we were all out of breath, and Caluso stopped running; Jose was sucking wind, as we all were. Jose was bent over, catching his breath, as he handed Caluso his handcuffs and said, "Put these on, or I'll fuckin shoot you right here." I burst out laughing. Caluso put the cuffs on.

Understand that Caluso and his crew knew all the detectives working on this case. He knew Jose and his brother Laz, so we were the ones who went to lock him up, we figured he wouldn't fight, and he didn't. He was very polite and acted like a complete gentleman, and we treated him well.

Whenever an opportunity presented for us not to have to fight a target, we would take full advantage of it; using your body as a battering ram or a linebacker takes its toll on you. We are all beat up now, but when you are young, you don't think you are damaging your body whenever you have to fight with one of these suspects.

When the rest of the crew was brought in later that night, it was like we were there with these guys; we were laughing about the bread truck. The Aardvark was like a celebrity. We never charged him with the theft of the bread truck, New York didn't care, and these guys were in enough trouble. We hit them when they had a whole pallet of Ketamine, "Special K,"

Caluso got eighteen years. They tied him to trying to kill a witness in one of the cases against him, the witness lived, and then they tried to kill him again—eighteen years in Federal prison. That's a long time. I learned a valuable lesson from this case; this case turned out to be a big deal; no one wanted to take the job. They thought it was a waste of time; I never shied away from a job after that, no matter how insignificant I thought it was, and I made a name for myself. I got the reputation of someone that you could rely on and that I would get the job done.

I had a similar situation; my Chief called me into his office and explained that he had ordered one of his Sergeants from one of the mid-level narcotics units to send his group out on surveillance and photograph all the drug dealers and gang bangers hanging around one of the Paterson Housing projects. He wanted everyone identified.

He told me he had asked for this six-month prior and had yet to see one photo. He asked if I wanted the job; I told him I did and needed three weeks to complete it. He was excited and asked what else I needed, and I told him I needed a certain

Detective from the Crime scene unit assigned to me until the job was finished. Done.

This Detective from the crime scene unit knew his stuff when it came to cameras and editing, I had trained him in the academy, and I nicknamed him "Face," He would make these crazy faces when I would make him do push-ups, "Face," was short for faces of death. That name stuck with him; he couldn't shake it.

A side note: I learned how to be a Police Academy Drill Instructor from an Academy Legend. This guy was a Rigger in the Marine Corps and had a bunch of HALO jumps. HALO stands for High Altitude Low Opening; he left the New Jersey State Police and began working with the Sheriff's Department. At the time, he was a Corporal and the funniest Drill Instructor I had ever worked with. Back in the day, you could say and do anything within reason and get away with it; the Academy was run like a Boot camp, not a college campus. So, Cpl. RW was yelling at a female recruit; she was a mess and needed to toughen up and get her shit together, Cpl. RW named her Nickels:

Cpl. RW: Do you know why I named you Nickels?

Nickels: Sir, no, Sir!

Cpl. RW: Cause your so goddamned ugly you look like you got beat over the head with a sock full of nickels!

Nickels: Sir, yes, Sir!

Officer Nickels proudly carried that nickname her whole career.

Face and I got all decked out in camo and snuck into this tree line on the edge of the housing project before the sun came up, I spotted for him, and he took the photos. The camera was so high-tech that we didn't need to be close. Face took some fantastic pictures; you could see the individual crack pieces in their hands and make out the denominations on the bills in their money wads. My buddy from high school owns a garbage company in Paterson, and he had the contract to empty the dumpsters on the property. They were so used to seeing his trucks in and out of there all day that it was business as usual when he would roll in. We sometimes rode along in the garbage truck and got super up-close photos.

We took all the pictures, Face cleaned them up, and printed them. We put the pictures in a photo album and took them to the Gang Intelligence Unit inside the jail. We asked them to identify everyone in our photo book. The Gang Intelligence Unit used their Jail informants and identified every person we photographed.

I took Face with me to see the Chief; we were a week ahead of schedule. The Chief was happy, finally results, Face did a great job, and he loved doing that kind of work. He got a little excitement out of it. Now that book became the basis for the giant raid that I spoke of prior in my story; that was the job that the SWAT team used me as a step stool.

Chapter 15

The travel trailer I bought was perfect; it was twenty-three feet long. The trailer was great for what I needed it for. I made it through the bulk of the winter and was ready to head down south.

This whole time, I let all the negativity from my AAD fire fester in my head. I allowed it in; these thoughts grew and morphed into false memories and twisting of reality. I started to doubt my skill and physical ability. I was afraid. Let me repeat that, I was afraid; I did not fear pain. I was already in pain. I live with pain daily; I have learned to ignore the pain. I do not fear death: I have now faced death three times. I don't want to die. I have learned to love life to appreciate life. Hell, I even celebrate my ability to brush my teeth and put socks on; I'm a simple man.

I was afraid of making a mistake, any mistake, I had upset many people, and all eyes would be on me. So, after breaking my neck and learning to do everything again, everyone scrutinized my every move. There was no way around it. I had to hold my head up and do the best I could, and hopefully, things would work out in the end.

My first stop was Skydive City, Zephyrhills, Florida, one of my favorite drop zones; I have always had a good time there; I met Bird Man Sam there. Sam Is a really good guy. When I was in the hospital, he called up the owner of the wingsuit rental company from which I had rented my suit. Sam worked out a fair price for me to pay for the wingsuit that I ruined. It was shredded, and the rental company was extremely reasonable. I paid them for the suit as soon as I got home from the hospital, but Sam didn't have to do that. I didn't even have to ask him. He just did it.

I was still trying to figure out what to expect when I got to Skydive City. Everyone calls Skydive City, Zhills. I got there and found a nice place to park my trailer. I had a few drinks and passed out. When I woke up the next day, I headed to manifest to check-in. In the back of my mind, I was worried they would not let me jump. I thought that they might not let me jump because of my accident. I checked in, and they told me I still had money in my account from 2021. They were as nice as ever, and they even remembered me.

So far, so good. I set my gear up where we always set up, and I settled in and sat there and watched the team from Qatar for a while. I was starting to relax; this is why I loved this place. I needed to build my confidence and stop being a whiny house mouse. Sam showed up, and we manifested ourselves on a load and started to suit up.

This is it. I'm doing this! We got on the plane and were going to do a track jump. It had been almost a year since I had done a track jump. I had no idea how my body would react or if I could hold the track position; screw it, let's do it!

We got to altitude, and we exited. I was stiff, but my exit was good. We were jumping out of an Otter, the door on the Otter was huge, so it was easy for me to have a stable exit. Sam was outside the door on the camera step to film my jump. The jump went great; as I said, I was worried about screwing something up. I was stiff, but I was stable; the moment of truth was coming,

Before I headed down to Zhills, I had to overcome the fear of my full-faced helmet and claustrophobia. I conquered the fear by wearing my helmet around my house for hours. I looked funny, but it was the only way to beat it.

My helmet altimeter began to beep; here we go! Stay calm; no need to rush. Stay stable. I reach back to grab my pilot chute. It's not there. I can't feel it, Instant Terror!

My mind races. All these scenarios instantly run through my brain. Go for your reserve, No! No! No! The pilot chute is there! Once I tell my brain that my pilot chute is there, I suddenly feel it. It is in my hand. It has been in my hand the entire time. It was all a mind game; I throw it, and my canopy opens. This whole scenario happened in a fraction of a second.

Now I know what to expect. My mind will fight me. It must be retrained; I know how to beat it now. I get into my landing pattern, and I stand my landing up.

JP, where do I begin?

JP was a Gulf War Veteran. He was an Air Force Military Police officer and became my partner after Jose was promoted and sent to narcotics. Everybody loved JP. He was so different from me; I was intense and quick-tempered, JP was mellow and laid back, we would laugh all day, and he broke everyone's chops relentlessly but not in a mean-spirited way. When JP was breaking your balls, you couldn't help but surrender and laugh cause if you didn't, it would just get worse. The best I can describe it was, If I found a magic lamp and the Genie gave me three wishes, I would have wasted one wish to have him stop breaking my chops!

During the winters, when it was just too cold to ride, we would double up in a car, and he would never drive; he said it was too much fun watching me hit everything with the car; he used to call me Magoo. He was right. I could ride the shit out of a bike but not so much in a car, two wheels good, four wheels bad!

141

We were driving up county on a 7 pm to 3 am shift, we had pissed our Sergeant off, and he had banished us to Dogwatch for a few tours. We were behind this vehicle that was all over the road, he turned into a residential neighborhood and started driving as if he lived there, making turns and such, so we decided to stay behind him for a little while to see where this would end up. Many drunk drivers turn into residential neighborhoods, sometimes pull into random driveways, and act like they are home. We also had a personal rule that we always followed; if we were behind a car and they made it home before we decided to turn our emergency lights on and pull them over, they were safe. No arrest.

We are following the vehicle, and he pulls into a driveway. Ok, let's see. The driver gets out of the car and starts walking to the house's front door, acting like he has no idea we are behind him. They always do that. Technically, he's safe, but we need to verify that he is home and read him the riot act, so he realizes how close he came to getting arrested. So, as he is walking to the front door, I call out to him, and he turns and looks at us; I put the spotlight beam directly on his head and tell him to come to the car. I loved doing that; it made my night. The driver walked to our car with the light beam on his head, and I always laughed so hard that I almost peed my pants.

The driver looked like he was getting abducted by Aliens as he walked into the beam; it is truly one of the funniest things you could ever see. We ID the driver and tell him how lucky he was; if he were drunker than the average bear, we would take his keys and leave them in dispatch for him to pick up the next day. This was in the mid-late '90s. We could give people breaks back then, but that changed after 2000.

After 2000-2001 there were no more breaks. It was a must-arrest scenario. One night we were driving through the town of

Clifton, N.J. we were stopped at a red light about five cars back when a vehicle came ripping past us in the right turn lane doing about 50 mph. I hit the lights and went after them. We pulled him over as they made the right-hand turn; I walked up to the driver's window, and as he rolled it down, the driver yelled." Go Rangers," Oh boy, here we go. It was 1997, and the New York Rangers had just won a playoff game. The driver was hammered, and I asked him to step out of the car; he was so happy he wanted to hug me. Rangers. Go Rangers! Ok, Sir, have a seat on the curb; hopefully, the passenger was sober.

He was asleep.

These two idiots lived three blocks away. Four hours of paperwork, $10,000 in lawyers' fees, court fees, and fines, not tonight. I throw the driver in the back of the patrol car; JP gets in the drunk driver's seat, drives the vehicle to the dude's house, wakes up his parents, gives them the keys, and we got out of there. As I said, we had discretion back then, and sometimes the best way to handle something wasn't an arrest. The following incident illustrates that point perfectly:

We were driving in Paterson, N.J., late one night when a car blew a red light right in front of us. JP blurts out, "Holy Red Light Runner!"

I look at him and say, "Who are you, fuckin Batman?"

JP says, "What? Go get them."

I tell him, "I can't believe you said something that stupid."

"Just go get them," he yells.

Lights on, here we go. We pull the car over, and I walk up to the driver's window and look inside with my flashlight; I look over the roof of the vehicle to get JP's attention, I want him to look inside the car, but he doesn't pick up on my hand gestures.

Sometimes JP was like that kid in little league baseball in the outfield throwing dirt bombs while the game was going on around him!

I asked the driver to please step out of the vehicle, then I said, "why don't we all step out of the vehicle." With that, out steps four mostly naked strippers from the Strip joint down the road; all they are wearing is unbuttoned flannel shirts; I just wanted JP to see what we were dealing with. Now, the driver had no license, none of them had a license, and they had no idea whose car it was. So here we are, standing on the side of the road, me, JP, and four naked strippers, and that's when it hit me. I had this vision of taking them into headquarters to figure this mess out and having every cop on duty make their way to the squad room, which could have turned into a giant can of worms. I envisioned the Squad room instantly transformed into a Go-Go Bar, Internal Affairs would have field day: it would be a nightmare.

So, we did the smart thing; we told them to have a great night, and we got out of there; sometimes, you must practice a little common sense and a lot of self-preservation. I did everyone on shift that night a huge favor. I loved working with JP. He was fun and loyal as hell.

One day, we walked into the motorcycle garage, and we ran into a friend of ours, another member of the Motorcycle Squad, Clark, affectionately known also as "Pumpkin Head," or "Head." His head was huge, about the size of, you guessed it, a pumpkin!

Me: What's up, Clark?

Head: That piece of shit, Jones. He's got me grabbing a car; then I have to go to his house; he has a groundhog trapped in one of those humane traps in his backyard. I have to take the trap up county and set the groundhog free. I'm not fuckin animal control.

We laughed and went our separate ways; two days later, we were in the Squad Room during lineup, and Sgt. Jones tells

144

Pumpkinhead to grab a car and take the trap up county again. He caught another groundhog. Clark looked pissed and did what he was told. We didn't think about it and went about our business.

Three or four days later, in Lineup, Sgt. Jones proudly states that he caught another groundhog. He must have a giant family of groundhogs living in his backyard. Lineup ends, and the Squad room clears out; I stop Head and pull him to the side; he's smiling.

Me: Head, what the hell is going on?

Head: What's going on? Every day I go to that scumbag's house, and I open the trap and let the groundhog out, I'm not his errand boy, and that stupid ass thinks he's got a family of groundhogs. I'll do this every day till I retire If I have to!

Now that is some good stuff, and stuff like this went on every day on the bikes. It was the funniest job I have ever had.

But there is always one, one person that has to ruin a good thing. We had one, and unfortunately, he was our Sergeant, Sgt. Jones (not his real Name). Sgt. Jones had it made; He oversaw one of the most prestigious units at the Sheriff's Dept; the hours were great, the equipment was top of the line, and the Sheriff assigned ten of the most squared away, aggressive officers in the entire department to the unit. Ten out of a thousand. The Squad ran itself, everyone on the squad got along well, and we all looked out for each other.

Jones went by many names, "Big Bird," also known simply as "the devil" or "El Diablo" and the "Yellow Motherfucker." I preferred Big Bird, he was about the same height and build as Big Bird, and he had this giant honker on his face and giant Rodeo Clown feet. I'm in no position to make fun of someone for their physical characteristics, but Jones was genuinely evil so why not.

Jones was highly insecure. He could not handle having a squad that got along and worked hard; he had to constantly try to stir up trouble between members of the Unit; he figured that if we all got along, we would somehow undermine his command. Foolish! We made him look good; if he had just concentrated on doing Admin work and having our backs, he would have been set.

Once Jose got promoted, I became Jones's biggest and most outspoken target, and it was only a matter of time before he knocked me off. Jones was powerful; as I said, we made him look good, and the Sheriff loved him, but we were also handpicked for the Unit, so there was a balance that needed to be struck, and when things were out of balance, everyone suffered.

Big Bird didn't need to catch you doing something wrong to have you knocked off. He required good timing and a few well-placed lies, and you were finished. The way it usually went down, they would knock you off; we called it the Wheel of Misfortune. Depending on how believable the lie was or how egregious your act of treason was, dictated your punishment, you could be destroyed and put back into the jail; if that happened, chances were that you weren't coming back, or you could get transferred back to regular Patrol. Depending on how you acted would dictate whether you revived yourself or not. You were never confronted on your supposed transgression; that didn't matter; what mattered was how you handled yourself.

We had just completed a funeral escort, and the entire squad was sitting at a giant table at the Pompton Queen Diner in Pompton Plains, N.J. We were the only uniformed unit allowed to eat lunch together, and we were gearing up when I got a call on the radio from the Patrol Sergeant. He ordered me to report to the Patrol Captain's Office immediately, I looked at Big Bird, and he wouldn't make eye contact with me. I said to him, "Looks like you finally got me." He looked down at his rodeo clown feet, speechless; what a coward.

I reported to the Captain's Office, Captain Viglione. Viglione was a decent guy; he didn't have much power, and he knew it, he would have your back the best that he could, but most things were out of his hands.

I walked into his office, he told me to sit down, and he began to explain to me that I was transferred to the 4 pm-12 pm shift, four days on, two days off; all my vacation days had been canceled, I needed to turn in my keys and clear out my locker in the motorcycle garage. He told me that I was not allowed to see the Sheriff and that he had no idea why this was happening, so don't ask him.

I told him that I was getting married in three weeks and my honeymoon was planned, Denied, and all my approved vacation days had been canceled. When they got you, they got you good. I cleared out my locker and dropped my keys off.

That Scumbag Big Bird finally got me; I was the number one producer on the bikes, all that hard work thrown away. I felt pretty much how I felt after my AAD fired and I was run out of the village.

I reported for duty two days later, and no one would stand next to me in Lineup, cowards. They knew Jones was a scumbag, but that's how it goes when you are on a knockoff. You become radioactive. I knew that I had done nothing wrong, but I wasn't going to try and explain anything to anyone, all eyes were now on me, and I couldn't trust anyone except JP; Jose wasn't around. I had to be careful. I knew if Big Bird just successfully got me, JP would be next. The problem was that JP didn't give a shit; he would wait for me to come in every day and make a scene. It usually went like this:

147

JP: "Hey, everyone, Gary's here; you remember Gary? He used to be your friend, you fuckin cowards!"

I would beg him to shut up before they got him next; he didn't care.

So, I made a decision. They wanted me to give up and bitch and moan. Poor me, they wanted me to stop working. They knew what I was capable of. If I shut down or complained they had me, Jones would win. I wasn't going out that way. Every day when I got out of Lineup, I would go to the Captain's Office. I would say the same thing every day. I would knock on his door, enter, and request permission to speak to the Sheriff. The answer was always the same, "Denied."

I wouldn't stick around headquarters. I had nothing to say to those cowards. I would hit the road and start working. When you're on the bikes, we had different expectations; Big Bird wouldn't let us come in at the end of the day unless we banged out twenty tickets, regardless of if you had arrests. Jones wanted twenty a day; on Patrol, they wrote twenty tickets a month.

I would hit the road and hunt; I wasn't going to upset the apple cart and start writing twenty tickets a night. I wasn't on the bikes anymore. I was looking for arrests, warrants, drugs, and stolen cars. I worked my ass off, My Sergeant was a good guy then, but he wasn't going near me either. The Sgt. would always call me on the radio when I was getting into stuff, he would ask if I needed any assistance, and I would always respond, "Negative, I'm good" I earned his respect. I never asked him for anything, and I was squared away; I was busy, I was on a mission, and this went on for four months. The same guys that wouldn't stand next to me in Lineup would come to me for help, help with complex accidents or DWI reports. I helped them because I had morals and honor.

148

About four months into my sentence, I was walking out of the restroom in the hallway near the entrance to the Patrol Division Headquarters; I walked right into the Sheriff, I saluted, and we saluted at the Sheriff's Department; it was very paramilitary. The Sheriff saluted back, and I thought, here is my chance. I asked the Sheriff if I could make an appointment to speak to him; I wasn't going down without a fight. The Sheriff looks at me and says, "get in my office,"

Here we go! This was going to be good, I walked into the Sheriff's Office, and he told me to sit down; I sat, and the Sheriff started talking; he was telling me how Sgt. Jones was his best Sergeant; he was letting me know to be careful, be very careful.

The Sheriff continues to say how Jones told him that I was the biggest troublemaker on the Motorcycle Squad. I looked at the Sheriff and said, "He's right; I am." It looked like I punched him in the face; the Sheriff said, "Officer's come in my office, crying, begging for mercy, and you sit here and tell me that you're the biggest troublemaker on the Squad."

I explained to the Sheriff, "I don't like Jones, I don't agree with how he treats his guys, but I'm loyal to you, and I always do my job!" The Sheriff looks at me and says, "You have balls, Pacelli. I like you; put Corporal stripes on your uniform; you're back on the bikes starting tomorrow, and you're second in command. But you must go to Jones's house when you leave here and let him know." I thanked him and left his office. I started laughing the second I got outside. You should have seen the look on Big Bird. It was worth the four months of humiliation. Jones Lost.

The Sheriff didn't get to be in his position by being stupid. He sent a clear message to Big Bird that day. I also realized something else that day. I realized that I was going to leave and get a job for another Department; I couldn't work for a Boss that would let one of his loyal guys rot the whole time, knowing it was over a lie. It was time for a change.

That day, the balance of power shifted a little; Big Bird was still very powerful, but he thought twice about messing with his guys and never messed with me again. He had no idea what went down in the Sheriff's office, he was blindsided by the Sheriff, making me a Corporal, and he was suddenly scared of JP, which was very bizarre.

The guys on the squad despised him and would do whatever they could to screw with him; I was amazed at how creative they were.

We had one guy that would constantly point the radar gun at him and turn it on; he thought maybe he could put him out of service.

One day, I walked into the motorcycle garage and saw JP polishing the seat on Jones's motorcycle. I watched for a minute, then asked him what he was doing? JP says he polished Big Bird's seat so that when he hit the brakes, he would slide forward and smash his balls against his bike's gas tank. I thought to myself how great of an idea that was.

Big Bird was on vacation; I watched Pumpkinhead take Jones's helmet off the hook, go outside, take a giant leak in his helmet, swish it around, and then leave it out in the sun to dry. For the rest of my time on the Bikes, whenever it was hot, and Jones would start sweating, he would say, "I smell Piss; do you smell Piss?" I know that is terrible, but hey, treat your guys better! Nobody ever pissed in my helmet.

They would constantly mess with his bike; I remember we were doing the Hawthorne Memorial Day Parade, and we pulled up; whenever we did a parade, Big Bird would get pissed and hammer us if we smiled or waved to the people watching the Parade. We never listened, but he always managed to make us miserable, so this day, we parked all lined up, and he broke out his tape measure to check our distance. He walks away. I see JP reach over, take the keys out of his bike, and throw them. Gone! When the parade started, Big Bird could not find his keys; He had to get a ride to the motor pool to get the spare set. The parade started, and we left him there. I don't feel bad; he ruined many people's careers without thinking twice.

On a funny note, everyone was tied up on other assignments, and I had to cover a traffic post. Jose was still on the bikes, and my partner at the time. The post was at the county parking garage across the street from the courthouse; at 3 pm, the courthouse would clear out, and a traffic officer was needed to clear out the garage. It was summer, sunny, and hot, just as I liked it. I was feeling good. I looked sharp, with motorcycle boots, riding britches, short sleeve shirt, helmet, and sunglasses. I took my post, was in great shape, and started directing traffic. I couldn't believe how receptive everyone was to me that day. Everyone was waving at me, beeping at me, and smiling at me. I couldn't believe how happy everyone was this fine summer afternoon. I directed traffic until the garage cleared out, and as I was wrapping up my post, Jose pulled up on his bike; he parked next to me and sat on his bike till I finished. I walked over to the bikes and said to him:

Me: Man, that was a great post; everybody was digging me! I had it going on!

Jose: No, you didn't jerkoff; your zippers down.

Me: What? God damn it!

I looked down, and there it was. My zipper was down.

I started laughing; how funny is that? I thought I was the shit.

We did have a good time on that squad, and what I wouldn't give to go back.

Chapter 16

"Whenever I think that I'm somebody, I'm easily offended;
then I realize that I'm no one, and I'm not offended anymore."
—Mike Tyson

I spent about three weeks in Florida at Skydive City, ZHills. I needed to see where I was physically; I knew where I was mentally; I was a mess. I had all winter to let it fester and grow. I had no confidence, I allowed the chirpers to get in my head, but they weren't the worst. The worst is when someone you consider a friend turns on you. You once valued their opinion, so when they say something, it has value, and those are the words that cause the most damage.

It's easy to ignore someone whom you don't have any respect for.

I was with Sam, I respected Sam, and Sam had no agenda. Sam will tell you like it is, good, bad, ugly.

The winds were unpredictable, and I got about fifteen jumps in.

I got run out of my home DZ and was treated like a hero at Zhills.

My story and video got around the drop zone, and people approached me and asked if I was the guy who broke his neck skydiving; some people wanted to jump with me, others wanted to help me if they could, and everyone was great. They couldn't believe I was jumping less than a year after my accident. They were amazed that I made it back to the drop zone, steering my canopy with my head, and that I didn't cry out or panic. No one criticized me for my body position or how fast I was going when I deployed. They even saw my AAD fire video and couldn't believe it, they acknowledged that I put myself in a bad position, but they also recognized how I didn't panic and stuck to my plan. No one judged me.

I met some incredible people; I met a jumper paralyzed from the waist down; he had the same injury as me, an incomplete spinal cord injury. He was injured from an IED in Afghanistan. I met the Skydiver on the cover of the Parachutist magazine; the cover picture was taken of him while he was swooping the pond. The cover photo captures the moment his prosthetic leg comes off as he skims the pond's surface; it is probably one of the best cover pictures ever taken.

I also met the "Naked Skydiver"; the naked skydiver holds the record for the most naked skydives in a day. Sixty-two, sixty-two naked skydives in one day, impressive and funny!

I met all these fantastic people. Being recognized for jumping and trying to get my life back felt good. I was tired of keeping my mouth shut, I needed work, but if I was coming back, this season was my last chance. Sam got me up in the air, but he was heading to Colorado, and I was heading to Skydive Shenandoah with a quick stop in South Carolina.

I left Skydive City feeling good about myself; the warm weather was doing wonders for my nerve damage. I still limped, the nerve pain was there, but I accepted it would always be there. I was going to be OK. I was looking forward to the long drive to South Carolina.

I stopped in South Carolina and got to see Lenny and his family; it was nice to see them, but I was starting to miss my own family, it was going on three weeks, and I still needed to stop at Skydive Shenandoah.

I parked the trailer at Skydive Shenandoah, and the season began; I met everyone that worked there, the Tandem Instructors, the pilots, manifest and everybody was pretty awesome; even the fun jumpers were excellent. I was anonymous, like a ghost; it was great. I needed to concentrate on putting my head back together, and Shenandoah was the place to do it. The air space wasn't crowded, and I could regain my muscle memory through repetition. I didn't have all eyes on me, waiting for one misstep or a simple mistake; working for Shauna was great. I could jump or not. I was working ground crew, so I was still training my body even if I didn't jump.

There is a Tandem Instructor there, Jungle George. Jungle George is a lot of fun. We have a lot in common; he is a retired Lieutenant from a narcotics unit, and we understand each other. He would convince at least one tandem student a day that I was Vin Diesel's stunt double. It was hilarious.

I could jump whenever I wanted to, but I found myself constantly looking for excuses to avoid jumping. I still had people living in my head rent-free.

My major problem was that I was a tracker. Tracking is a type of Skydiving, like belly or angle flying. In the plane, there is an exit order that is standard around the world, it changes slightly, but the exit order is usually the same everywhere.

Moving groups go first or last. Tracking is a moving group. Tracking is wing suiting without a wingsuit. You don't go as fast or as far, but you still get moving quickly. When you track, you are not falling straight down. You are moving horizontally as you are falling.

I track because I have a lot of trouble doing a belly jump. After all, I cannot arch my back. The tracking position is perfect because I am wired and fused together. I am like a lawn dart, and I can track almost a mile and a half, depending on how low

I deploy my canopy. I usually track around a mile and start to slow down at 6,500 ft, depending on the winds, I usually open at 4,500 ft, very conservative.

Since I had to get out first, I had to sit on the floor, the plane was always crowded, and I usually couldn't get a seat on the bench. I was self-conscious about sitting on the floor because I wasn't that limber, and it took me longer to get up and open the door. Then, I would rush my exit and blow it because I was unstable.

I would rush because if you take too long setting up in the door, you are screwing the skydivers in the back of the plane. You may put them in a bad spot, and they may not make it back to the drop zone and land off.

Since at most drop zones, trackers get out either first or last, Shauna started allowing me to get out last, and then I had no more excuses, but I sometimes still needed a kick in my ass to get me on the plane, and that's where Erin came in.

I met Erin at the beginning of the season. She was one of those super Ninja Tunnel Fliers, she was a damn good skydiver, and she motivated me to get on the plane and jump! That's what I was there for, wasn't it?

Everybody was cool at Shenandoah. They were all very patient with me and would help me whenever I needed it. I met some great people there; I would love to name them, but I didn't get their permission, but they know who they are.

I loved working the ground crew; Shauna hooked me up. The work was perfect for me, even though it wasn't physical work for a normal person; at that point in my recovery, it was a lot. I was like a newborn baby. My muscles were like an old battery that couldn't hold a charge. The work was very physical for me, but it felt fantastic. I had the Sun beating down on me; it felt great.

The way the plane loading area is set up at Skydive Shenandoah, you were right in the middle of the action; the plane loaded right in front of the hanger, so you never missed a beat.

What I loved most was seeing and interacting with all the first-time tandem students. I loved the energy; I loved fist-bumping everyone boarding the plane. I could have jumped more than I did, but I had too much fun loading the plane.

Everybody was so cool, and they all treated me well; there was no drama, at least none that involved me or that I noticed. Everything about Shenandoah was good for me. The place, the people, the Vibe, everything. It was exactly what I needed.

When I was on the motorcycle squad, we could break away from the inner city now and then. We would ride Up-County, into the most rural part of the county, set up on some deserted County Road, and run radar; we would never write speeding tickets. The Sheriff found out that Big Bird was making us write twenty tickets a day, so he had warning books printed for us, and he told Big Bird that they counted the same as tickets. The Sheriff was brilliant. His department wasn't getting the revenue from the tickets anyway, and these people were his voters, so he certainly didn't want to make them angry.

We would run Radar all day on this deserted road and write speeders warnings. They loved us; they would get out of their cars and check out our bikes. It was just a way to chill out and enjoy a hot summer day. We were young, and I would love to stand on the road and feel the heat rising, and I would breathe in that diesel asphalt smell, and I felt like I was part of the street; I can't explain it any better, but I always missed that after I left that squad, but I found it in Shenandoah, it brought back that memory. I could stand there on the tarmac or runway and experience the same feeling of the heat rising and the asphalt smell. I loved it.

When the season started, I couldn't jump because it was too cold, then I started getting out low, doing Hop N Pops, and asking the Pilot to let me out higher and higher. I had a slow beginning, but I didn't care. I was jumping.

I had a great summer; September hit, and I started to notice the change in the air, and the temperature started to drop; when October hit, I would have to go in my trailer as soon as the sun went down. The temperature would fall so fast. My trailer was perfect for me, but it was on the small side; it was perfect when I could hang out after the sun went down and then go in my trailer when it was time to sleep.

When I went into the trailer at sundown, it was way too long to be in that small of a space, so I had to pack up and head out about three weeks before they shut down for the season.

I finished up the season at Skydive Sussex, and I was worried about how I would be received. I worried for nothing, everyone was happy to see me, and I was glad to see them. Skydive Sussex was my home DZ before my accident, and it is a lot busier than Shenandoah. I wanted to make sure I had my shit together before jumping in the ring; everything moves faster there.

I finished the season with some fantastic jumps. I did a bunch of High pulls; it was the first time I had ever done a high pull. A few times, I would get out last and track. I would follow the plane out and deploy my canopy at 6,500 ft and sit up in my harness and let the wind fly me back to the drop zone. I loved it; I hit my 400th jump there.

I was free, and my mind was clear. I had my confidence back and felt so grateful. This time I knew how I was able to make it happen. I knew God was in control; I was doing a front ride. I was doing a front ride, and God was my Tandem Instructor. Every jump I do now is just a front ride with God flying.

I have changed everything. I have completely changed the way I think about Skydiving. I finally get it and no longer chase numbers; I take myself off the load if the weather isn't good. A few times, when I pulled myself off a load due to the winds, someone took my lead and got off also. Nobody wants to be first; I'll be; I will be a leader, not a follower. I don't care; there is always another load. I learned I want to enjoy my jumps, not just survive them. When I get to the DZ, If I'm not feeling it, I wait. I don't rush, and I don't explain anything. If I don't feel like jumping, it's nobody's business. I also changed out my lines, I try only to use Dacron lines. I read a stat that most fatal accidents of jumpers over sixty were the result of hard openings, and most could have been prevented by using Dacron. Dacron has a little give to it. I'm not sixty yet, but I'll take every advantage I can get.

What's important? Skydiving? Relationships? Family and friends? The answer to all these questions is yes. I break skydiving up into individual adventures. I have learned from losing the ability to jump that the whole process is sacred to me, and I want to squeeze every ounce of joy out of every part of my jump.

It begins with planning, and it is just like Detective work. We do an OPS plan. I wake up early and do my "winds" I get the winds from my weather App. And I plan out the day, where I will open my Canopy, and where I will start my landing pattern. And much more, then you check your gear, no different from being on patrol. Suit up, and board the plane. The excitement inside me is building, sitting on the plane, climbing to altitude. I like to sit in silence and look out the window. You check your gear for the third or fourth time and look around the plane at other jumper's rigs to see if anything seems out of place.

At Skydive Sussex, Paul, the Pilot, rings the Cow Bell when we are two minutes out. Then the door opens, I close my visor, jumpers start to exit, slide down the bench, check the spot, make sure my air space is clear, set up in the door, and exit. The moment my foot breaks contact with the plane, another part of my jump begins, and I experience new and different scenarios and events. Approximately sixty seconds of freefall, and then you deploy your Canopy. This is the part I love the most, flying your Canopy or even just pulling down the leg straps on your rig, this allows you to sit in your harness like a chair, and you just let the wind float you back to the drop zone. It is incredible how beautiful it is up there, and it is so quiet you can hear the silence; that's when I appreciate all the gifts and chances I have received.

Landing your Canopy is the icing on the cake. It was the most satisfying thing I have ever experienced when I could stand up my landings. It would be like bowling a strike or making that unbelievable putt on the golf course. I plan to consistently stand my landings up if I keep training and slowly recovering. Not standing my landings up does not take anything away from my Jumping experience. Standing the landing up just adds that much more pleasure to the jump.

I usually land last, I mostly exit last, and I will stay in brakes and let the wing suiters land before me. This way, I can take my time in the landing area and not worry about being in anyone's way or possibly getting hit by another jumper. The field, for me, is incredible! The sun, and the smell of the grass, I love it.

I take my time to compose myself; I'm not embarrassed to say it, but sometimes I am overwhelmed by being able to skydive. Laying in that backyard in North Carolina, unable to move and now being able to jump is a big deal to me. Losing all hope, trying to fuckin swallow my tongue, planning on driving a motorized wheelchair in front of a bus, not being able to pee, having nurses wipe my ass and feed me. Yeah, sometimes I tear up and must take a minute to compose myself; I'm baring my soul. Make fun of me if you want. I'll even help you. I have been through absolute hell and back.

On three occasions, I was so close to death that I could smell its breath. I was imprisoned in my own body, I was angry, bitter, and void of any hope. My fucking dog died while I was in the hospital,

Yes, I have earned the right to be treated with respect, not to be harassed or made fun of. I don't want to hear it anymore. Some people had decided that I would never be able to skydive again. They were wrong, and they need to accept that and be happy for me or leave me alone, but if they can't, have at it; it only makes them look small and petty. None of the chirpers have any power over me anymore. I genuinely feel sorry for them. I am free.

I take extra time in the field to compose myself and enjoy the moment. I have learned that breaking my neck and damaging my spinal cord was a horrific, unfortunate accident that has permanently disabled me. I can walk around like a victim and spout that poor me nonsense, or I can see it as an incredible gift. I have been allowed to learn the secret. It is so simple; we can all know and live by it.

The secret is to treat people with respect and dignity and to help each other; consider others before yourself, set an example, and stand by your convictions and beliefs. This accident has changed me in many ways, and I can choose to be happy and friendly to people just as quickly as I can choose to be angry and mean to people. This doesn't imply that I'm here to take anyone's abuse, but it does mean that I'm not going to give anyone any abuse. All of that is unnecessary. We have to start looking out for each other, even people we don't know. It is a mindset and lifestyle, and I choose to help people. I have been given incredible gifts that I want to share; they are free!

I jump alone. This upsets some people. I will jump with people at times, but I mostly jump alone. It's not personal, I have been through a lot, and I want to absorb every part of my jump. I take everything in; since my accident, I have jumped with very few people, Shauna, Sam, Rich, Erin, and Dario. Everyone I used to jump with has advanced to the next level; it's great to see.

All said and done, I jumped seventy-five times that first season back.

Chapter 17

I'm eighteen years old, and I walk into the military recruiting office in Pompton Lakes, New Jersey; I enter the first door. I think it was the Army. I ask: What branch has the longest boot camp? Marines, third door on the right.

I walked into the United States Marine Corps recruiting office, or "the third door on the right," at the time; they both had about the same amount of meaning to me.

Me; I heard the Marines have the longest boot camp.

Cpl. Spellman: yes, we do. What are you interested in doing?

Me: The toughest job that you have

Cpl. Spellman: Infantry, when would you want to leave?

Me: As soon as possible.

And that was the easiest sell Cpl. Spellman ever had.

Two months later, I was on a bus in Beaufort, South Carolina, sitting next to this pain in the ass that wouldn't stop talking. This magic bus I am riding is taking me to the rest of my life; it is magical because the Gary Pacelli sitting in it is about to be transformed, born again hard!

The bus stops, we are getting screamed at, we exit the bus, and I see them, a stargate to a new life, a life of purpose. The footprints, I stand on the mythical yellow footprints, and I wait:

Nothing! Nothing happened; what the hell? Wasn't I supposed to be transformed? Oh. Do you mean I have to earn it and put the work in? I see.

After some more screaming and organized chaos, we are told to enter the building; above the door is a sign it reads:

Through this portal shall pass the world's fiercest fighting force!

I vowed that the only way I would leave that Island was a Marine or dead.

You joined the Army.

You become a Marine!

I passed through the portal; that's a door for everyone who isn't in the Navy or a Marine. I took well to the structure and discipline of Marine Corps boot camp. I was a squad leader for a day until my senior Drill Instructor fired me for marching like a duck, but that was ok because they then coronated me as "The King of the Land of the Midgets." I was finally recognized for my excellence. The Staff Sgt. declared that since I was the tallest, short person in the Platoon, I was responsible for anyone shorter than me. Whenever one of my loyal subjects fucked something up, I was responsible, and I would pay along with the violator. It seemed fair to me; it was only natural that I took full responsibility for my kingdom and my loyal subjects. I loved the insanity of it all, all the madness; it all had a purpose.

Once we got through receiving and had our heads shaved, we all looked the same. After a few weeks, I realized that my bunkie was the "pain in the ass" on the bus who wouldn't stop talking. He had the top bunk; he was cool as hell.

I remember when I got "Dear John'd," I was on my way back from a dentist appointment, walking past the mess hall, and no one was around. I had a pass to call my parents to give them information on my transportation arrangements after graduation. I was an 84-day reservist since I was in college; I had to report to my duty station the day after I graduated. My family had planned on driving down and driving me back. Anyway, I had a pass to use the pay phone, and since I had not received any letters from my girlfriend, I snuck a call into her house.

Big Fuckin Mistake! Her little sister answered the phone and asked me why I was calling; her sister had a new boyfriend now. She proceeded to tell me his name; it was one of my best friends! This is getting good, her mother got on the phone, and she was charming, but her daughter refused to get on the phone. After a bit of them yelling back and forth at each other, she got on the phone and told me to fuck off, and hung up. I'm not sure if those were her exact words, but it was her exact meaning. Excellent, good times were had by all.

I got back to my Squad Bay and was checked out. What a kick in the gut; my Bunkie, Bobby, took one look at me and knew I was about to blow. He got together a few of my buddies, and they gave me an ultimatum, I had that night to get my head back in the game, or they were going to drag me into the shower and beat my brains in. I had other things to worry about, and if A Drill Instructor found out what happened, I was a dead man.

They were right; I had more important things to worry about, the here and now. I cleared my mind, pushed it down deep, and embraced the suck, and that was the moment that I was " born again hard."

I put it out of my mind and became hardcore. I had nothing holding me back; the Drill Instructors couldn't touch me; I didn't care, and when you don't care, you become powerful and dangerous. I put my heart and soul into boot camp, and the days flew by. I only thought about this again two weeks before I graduated.

We were finishing up ICT, Individual Combat Training; ICT has been replaced now by "the Gauntlet."

We were in the field, and they were doing mail call; I wasn't paying attention because I had yet to get a letter since boot camp started, maybe one in the beginning.

The Drill Instructor called my name; as I said, I wasn't paying attention. He called it again, and then I heard it the third time, but it was too late. I was paying for this, so after about a thirty-minute lesson in the art of "pain compliance," I got my letter and returned to where I was sitting with Bobby.

I sat there staring at the envelope; I couldn't believe she had written me a letter. I couldn't imagine what else needed to be said. Bobby looks at the envelope and says, "is that from her?" He snatches it out of my hands and quickly rips it up. I couldn't believe what had just happened and being that I had just been trained in "pain compliance," I punched him right in his head, and it was on! We started rolling around in the dirt; we beat the hell out of each other till we both started laughing hysterically.

What Bobby did for me was huge; what good could come from reading that letter? I never looked back. The Drill Instructors didn't find any humor in our situation. Here we are, ten days in the field, and we just beat the snot out of each other. We were about to graduate, and now the Drill Instructors spent the next few hours putting us through what they thought was hell. They didn't realize yet, that we had graduated already in our minds; there was nothing they could do to us. We smiled through it all; finally, the Senior figured out that we were beyond his reach; we would die before we quit. They gave up, and I never did another push-up on Parris Island. I was a Marine!

I have been putting the work in since I stood in those footprints a lifetime ago!

I realize, looking back, that I have the power over my thoughts, and if I can re-train my brain to walk and hold a fork and get dressed, I can undoubtedly re-train my brain to flush out the negative things that people say or do to me. If I don't let them get in my head, there is room for positive thinking, and I have learned not to take the gifts I have been given for granted.

The quote from Mike Tyson makes so much sense when you break it down.

"Whenever I think that I'm somebody, I'm easily offended; then I realize that I'm no one, and I'm not offended anymore."
—Mike Tyson

Whenever I get prideful and arrogant, I get offended when people are rude or say stupid things to me. We start to become these self-centered, self-important people. We allow people to dictate how we feel. We give them power over our thoughts by letting them get inside our heads. We believe we are more important than we are. We rush around like the balance of the world is resting on our shoulders with our little conference calls or meetings. When we sit down and think about what we are accomplishing, we realize how insignificant we and our plans are.

Mike Tyson said that when he realizes he is no one, he is no longer offended. He released himself from feeling "offended" or angry and is now free to experience life. How many of us experience life? I mean, take life in; try it one day. Take a day and stop and think about everything you do. Start when you open your eyes in the morning, then when you put your feet on the ground, when you walk into the kitchen and pour yourself a cup of coffee, turn your laptop on, check your phone, pet your dog, kiss your spouse! I think you understand. I couldn't do any of those things. There are people right now who cannot do any of those things, and there are people we know that are deceased who cannot do those things. How valuable are these things to you now? Am I making my point?

We think we are so clever, all our carefully laid out plans and schemes; we think we are going places. We ask God for help when we need it, then forget about him until we get ourselves

166

in trouble again. I'm not standing here on my soap box preaching. I'm probably one of the worst offenders.

Mike Tyson has another quote:

"Everyone has a plan until they get punched in the face."
—Mike Tyson

I have lived by that quote my whole life, but when I was floating around those five minutes, staring at death, I realized how insignificant my plans were. I had plans, and there were things that I was working on. I was jumping so much because I wanted to hit my five hundred jumps to get my "D" license and become a Tandem Instructor. I got "punched" in the face, and those plans instantly disappeared. I realized that no matter what happened to me, the world would keep turning, and life would go on without me, and that's when I realized how small I was.

I have been blessed with a miraculous recovery. Every doctor I see, and I see a few, always tells me that I have had a miraculous recovery. It's a miracle, they say. It may be. A more immense blessing to me isn't the physical recovery but the lessons learned. You can't pay for that kind of knowledge; to me, that is the true gift.

Don't get me wrong, I wish that my accident had never happened, but I'm not going to waste the gifts given to me; instead, I will embrace my newly found knowledge rather than worry about the pain and loss of mobility that I have. I could be dead or paralyzed, but I'm not.

The physical recovery was unimaginable. I knew that if I stayed positive and believed, and I mean believed, with every atom in my body and every thought in my head, God would heal me, I had to "put the work" in, but more importantly, I had to believe. Putting the work in and the intensity which I put in

167

the work correlates with how much I believe. So, if I half-assed my therapy and went through the motions, wouldn't that express that I didn't believe? I will keep it simple. Your mind is very powerful, and staying positive is the key; it is hard; your brain is like your muscles and needs training. Keeping a positive mindset has to be a lifestyle.

Some people call it the universe. This is not a theological debate. You do you, I'm going to do me, and we don't have to debate, fight or argue. The most amazing thing about Skydiving is that you have all different people of all races, religions, backgrounds, and wildly different personalities together enjoying their passion, sitting around a firepit after an incredible day of Skydiving. Everyone is sharing a drink, laughing, and having a great time enjoying everyone's company. Everyone is welcome. I have never experienced that in all my days anywhere else. It is the norm on any Drop Zone that I have visited. The world can learn a few things from Skydivers.

I know that I will have to overcome hardships in life, but at least I will have the opportunity.

I will face physical pain and limitations; I will ignore the pain, adapt, and not be put in a box.

I decide what I do, I choose when I skydive, and no one is better than anyone else; like when I was in boot camp, we are all equally worthless in the big picture, and the more I understand how worthless I am, the more valuable I become.

I will act with courage and honor, no matter how others act.

I will treat everyone with respect and dignity, whether they deserve it or not.

I will be thankful for what I have,

I live by a code; I follow the core beliefs of courage, truth, honor, discipline, and perseverance. Reverence for God is central in my life, and I respect both my friends and my enemies. I will stand up for what I believe in and whom I care and have respect for.

I didn't invent this code; this code was the Viking Code of Honor and is similar to the Knight's code of Chivalry. These codes were intended to keep all that followed them in agreement with each other, on and off the battlefield. Following these codes made individuals act honorably and civilized, allowing them to function in modern society.

I thoroughly believe, with all my soul, in what I am attempting to accomplish, and I know that when I emerge on the other side, I will be bloodied, but I will be Victorious; I will succeed, or I will die trying. Would you be willing to die for something you didn't believe in?

That would be stupid!

Belief or Faith in God and oneself are essential. Just like the recruits in the academy, we sell ourselves short. We underestimate our ability to persevere in extreme hardship, but we are not alone!

Backup is available!

We need to ask for it and believe.

I wish I could stress enough or write more convincingly, but there is absolutely no doubt in my mind that God has saved me many times, and we need to clear our minds, so we can hear God; he speaks to us; we just need to listen.

Never give up, never give in, and never leave anyone behind! Thank you for your time.

Blue Skies
Gary Pacelli
The short and furious!

Photos

"It is not death that a man should fear, but he should fear
never beginning to live."

— Marcus Aurelius,

To see videos of my accident, AAD Fire, and return jump
landing go to YouTube:

Accident Video:
https://youtu.be/73tv4KMKcVs

Return jump Landing:
https://youtube.com/shorts/6KJDx5bDjeg?feature=share

AAD Fire:
https://youtu.be/cuJN7PK8qWU

Track Jump with Dario at Skydive Sussex

Skydive City, Zephyrhills, Florida

Skydive Sebastion

Whiskey

Gunner

Santa, JP and me

The Exoskeleton Suit

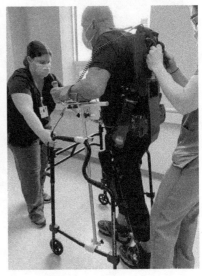

220 Kilos of Cocaine, courtesy of Detective Jerry Speziale.

Jose with 18,000 bags of Heroin

Lenny, Jose, Derin, Casey and me

Me and Kristin

Night, ice dive, February 1995

Me, Shauna and the Shark, on Return jump at Shenandoah.

My lead physical and occupational
Therapists.

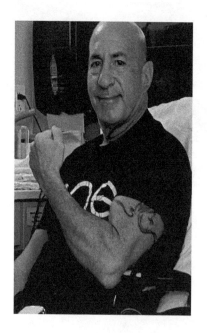
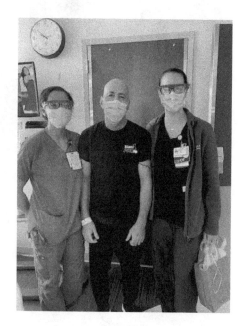

Money, money, and money   Me and my niece.

Lenny, Jose, Joe, Mel & Jimmy

Polar Bear Plunge Jenkinson's Bar

Skydive City, FL   Me & Sam at Shenandoa

USMC

This is my Ladder, there are many like it but this one is mine!

Short and Furious!

Jump 400

I had a good run!

Flight Pattern – March 9. 2021

The Accident

Combat Cross and the Legion of Honor

Wanaque PD with JP

PCSD Motorcycle Squad

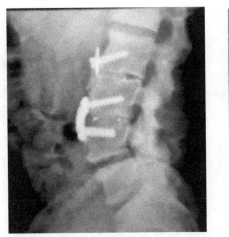

Back

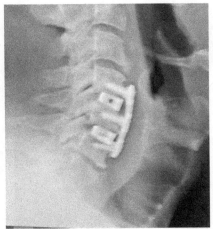

Neck

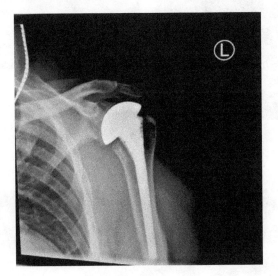

Shoulder

I am Iron Man! Actually I'm, Titanium Man.

Whiskey

Sam Kidstar- The Birdman

Before & After

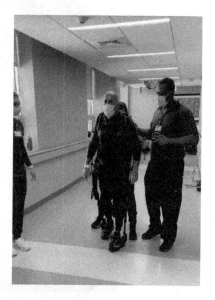

Walking out of the hospital

Me and Big Rich (Pop Low)   Veterans day jump 2019

ZHills

Money & Drugs

My wife .... My rock

About the Author

Gary Pacelli was a career Law Enforcement Officer who attended the Corrections Officer Academy and the Police Officer Academy. Gary has worked in every level of Law enforcement, from working in a County Jail, Municipal Police Officer, Municipal Detective, County Patrol Officer, Motorcycle Officer then County Detective. While he was a County Detective, he was assigned to the Passaic County Prosecutors Gang and Drug Task force while simultaneously assigned to the Drug Enforcement Administration. He was a Sheriff's Emergency Response Team (SERT) member, a Police Diver, a Police Academy Physical Fitness Senior Training Advisor, and an Academy Drill Instructor. Upon his retirement, he worked for the FBI as an Investigative Specialist, and Gary is also a certified commercial diver and a United States Marine.

Gary Was awarded two of the highest commendations in Law Enforcement, The Legion of Honor and the Combat Cross.

Gary is an active Skydiver and is involved in the Skydiving industry as Chief of Ground Operations at Skydive Shenandoah at the New Market Airport in New Market, Virginia. He lives in the Hudson Valley region of Upstate New York with his beautiful wife, two kids, and two dogs, Whiskey and Hennessy.

Printed in the USA
CPSIA information can be obtained
at www.ICGtesting.com
LVHW101103170823
755276LV00002B/277